The Strait Gate
Entrance To Life
By
Peter Mathias

THE STRAIT GATE: ENTRANCE TO LIFE
PETER MATHIAS

Published By Parables
October, 2018

All Rights Reserved. No part of this book may be reproduced or utilized in any form or by any means, electronic or mechanical, including photocopying, recording, or by any information storage and retrieval system, without permission in writing from the author.

ISBN 978-1-945698-72-9
Printed in the United States of America

Readers should be aware that Internet Web sites offered as citations and/or sources for further information may have been changed or disappeared between the time this was written and the time it is read.

The Strait Gate
Entrance To Life
By
Peter Mathias

PUBLISHED by PARABLES
Earthly Stories with a Heavenly Meaning

Chapter 1
FUNDAMENTAL DOCTRINE

Matthew 7: 13- 14 Enter ye in at the strait gate, for wide is the gate, and broad is the way that leadeth to destruction, and many there be which go in there at; Because strait is the gate, and narrow is the way, which leadeth unto life, and few there be that find it.

The Christian faith is about salvation and eternal life in Christ, yet these things are not the primary concerns of many converts these last days. Maybe because of anxieties, worries, and troubles of this life; I don't know what other preachers think or have to say about church and salvation in this new age. It is obvious the comforts of this life and values of this sinful world are actually taking over the place of salvation in the hearts of many converts, these modern days. I understand a lot of preachers are very much comfortable with this modern development. In this present generation, it appears the church is very much anxious about earthly glory and splendor, giving little attention to ultimate purpose of salvation which is about eternal life in Christ Jesus.

Frankly speaking, a whole lot of preachers in this modern era of church business are not after salvation and eternal life. Many run after earthly treasures and seek the praise of men. Could this be as a result of the strong influence of material mammon these last days or what? In these modern days, financial success and material possessions are the ultimate goals of many modern preachers as if Christ redeemed the church by means of offering money for our salvation. Christ Jesus did not offer money to anyone for the saving of our souls. He offered Himself as sacrificial Lamb and was crucified for the saving of all humankind. What does He expect from us, His church? Christ expects His church to conform properly to basic doctrine. The teaching of God's kingdom, salvation, and divine grace (gospel) as distinguished from Moses' law, directs every convert towards the strait gate and narrow way which leads to everlasting life.

The Christian faith does not by any means esteem material mammon, values of this life, or earthly treasures above heavenly treasures. The doctrine of Christ strongly emphasizes about eternal life above everything in this life. The Christian faith effectually upholds the fundamental doctrine of Christ Jesus which strongly reveals His innate nature and supernatural behavior.

1 Timothy 6:7 For we brought nothing into this world, and it is certain we can carry nothing out.

Christians who appreciate this spiritual truth, as reveal in 1st Timothy 6:7 don't hesitate to follow the narrow way which leads to the exceptional peace, joy, and fulfillment every true convert desire in Christ.

In Christian living and pursuit of God's kingdom, understanding holiness of Christ is priority and very much important. Without holiness no man shall see the Lord. The primary purpose of church existence in this world is to carry out the great commission even as the Christian grow daily in sanctification through faith in Christ Jesus.

Hebrews 12: 14 Follow peace with all men, and holiness without which no man shall see the Lord.

Holiness of Christ is a lifestyle. It is an awesome and an outstanding heavenly lifestyle originating from God. The Christian conforms to this heavenly heritage daily in the fear of the Lord and with total submission to yearnings of the Holy Spirit. Though somewhat difficult to explain however, this heavenly heritage is not a religious formality and is not by human effort but the work of the Holy Spirit and begins with the heart.

Salvation of the Christian is the work of the Holy Spirit and it begins with the inward thereby, manifesting outwardly through good works, actions and sober conduct. This simply means, holiness is not just an outward separation from sin alone; the Christian has strong relationship with Christ, and it is the work of the Holy Spirit from the inward. Holiness is about mercy, forgiveness, grace, selflessness, contentment, obedience to God, gratitude towards God, longsuffering, self control, sobriety, meekness, and fear of the Lord; and not just an outward separation from the world and sin alone.

I can't tell how other preachers and converts in today's church understand holiness. But I wouldn't forget the Bible revealing holiness as the innate characteristics of the Almighty God. Holiness is a supernatural behavior originating from God. It begins with the heart when it involves the Christian. The attributes of this heavenly heritage is found in the primary teachings of Christ Jesus. Beginning with the book of Matthew chapter five to chapter seven; in Matthew chapter 5, chapter 6, and chapter 7, Christ unveiled basic doctrine which depicts true holiness and saving faith. Mark, Luke, and John also unfold same fundamental doctrine.

Exodus 34: 6 And the Lord passed by before him, and proclaimed the Lord God, merciful and gracious, longsuffering and abundant in goodness and truth.

The above scripture says God is merciful, gracious, patient, abundant in goodness and truth.

Exodus 34: 6 reveals five major attributes which unveil the holiness of God. These attributes were what Jesus of Nazareth manifested in this world before He ascended into the heavens.

Exodus 34: 6 truly unveil the innate nature and supernatural behavior of the Almighty God. Man was made to bear that strong spiritual resemblance to God, and man was holy to God before the fall [Genesis 1:26]. After the fall, Adam lost that spiritual resemblance which he inherited from God and holiness disappeared out of human race. The sin nature which all mankind inherited from Adam influences people to sin every day. It negatively affects people's mind and understanding so they cannot perceive the mercy of God and repent of their ways.

All thanks to God Almighty, which hath made us meet to be partakers of the inheritance in light: who hath delivered us from the power of darkness and hath translated us into the kingdom of His dear Son; in whom we have redemption through His blood, even the forgiveness of sins [Colossians1: 12-14].

The Christian is transformed and regenerated through Christ, though flesh continue to operate within us and we cannot eradicate our sin nature, but we can allow the Holy Spirit to lead or control us so that we do not give in to desires of the flesh.

Regaining holiness to mankind was victoriously accomplished by Christ Jesus on day of His resurrection. After the resurrection of our Lord Jesus Christ, holiness is being constantly developed in the process of sanctification through the Holy Spirit, and we shall resemble Christ in full spiritual likeness when the Church is glorified.

Roman 8: 30 moreover, whom He did predestinate, them He also called, and who He called, them He also justified, and whom He justified, them He also glorified.

John 15: 14 Ye are my friends, if ye do whatsoever I command you.

When Christ ascended into the heavens, He did not leave His church without doctrine to follow. He provided sound doctrine and expects us to conform to

His sound doctrine. This is what the Christian faith stands for; total conformity to teachings of Christ. It is all about the strait gate and the narrow way which leads to life. Christianity is about complete submission to Christ and His teachings.

To be precise, faith without conforming to the teachings of Christ is not genuine, but hypocritical and worthless. Secondly, faith without submitting to the yearnings and leading of the Holy Spirit may amount to no reward after the race on the last day. The fear of the Lord is what actually keeps faith alive and obedience to God's word is what guarantees eternal life. One cannot have saving faith outside the fear of the Lord and total conformity to teachings of Christ.

It's so funny and at same time very unpleasant seeing traditions of men, negative civilizations of this world, human ideas and all sorts of worldliness have stronger influence in the church of God, while fundamental doctrine is being neglected and forsaken. Instead of the church making impact in the world, the system is the one now making so much impact in the church and holiness is nowhere to be found among many modern converts. No happening of this life takes the Almighty God unaware. He sees the end of everything before the beginning of all things.

Therefore, the scripture is fulfilled in this modern generation.

By strictly looking into Christ' doctrine, I understand very well that life does not end to this present sinful world. There is life after this natural life on earth. Eternal life is real and eternal damnation or everlasting punishment is also real. The influence of this present material world in church these last days is so much. It is not something the Christian should ignore or over look. The Christian faith is not about values and cultures of this life, but about heavenly treasures and everlasting life in Christ. Obedience to God's command through Christ is saving faith and assurance of salvation.

Overcoming the strategies of anti Christ in today's church will only take complete submission to basic doctrine of Christ Jesus. True Christians conform daily to His fundamental doctrine. In such conformity lies the assurance of salvation. Through knowledge from God's word, I understand very well that conforming to primary teachings of Christ Jesus such as, seek ye first the kingdom of God, and His righteousness "Matthew 6: 33" is what actually prepares one for God's kingdom.

As a kid, many years back, whenever I step my feet into the sanctuary of worship, what comes to my mind is heaven. Maybe because there was nothing to worry about or because I have heard the priest preached about heaven several times. Many adults go to the sanctuary of God consistently but without heaven at heart. While others go to church with one ulterior motive or the other. Some still allow the fear of the Lord to overwhelm them despite anxieties and worries of this life. Christ expects us to seek His kingdom consistently above all things no matter the troubles of this world.

In the other words, salvation and eternal life should be the ultimate purpose of going to church despite the temptations of this life which confronts the Christian on daily basis. If not, the flesh may want to take advantage of these troubles and thereby, overpower the soul, and rule over the Christian through anxieties, pains and worries of this life. The ultimate purpose of salvation is everlasting life in Christ not comforts of this world and vanities of this life.

Matthew 10: 38 And he that taketh not his cross, and followeth after me, is not worthy of me.

The closest enemy of the human soul is flesh. Flesh has ruined countless number of souls in this world after the fall of man in Eden. Nevertheless, the Christian strives daily to yield to yearnings of the Holy Spirit without hesitations. When the flesh is subdued and kept under control, Satan is rendered handicapped and frustrated to a reasonable extent. We are in the world, but not of this world. True Christians understand very well the ultimate purpose of salvation, and take their pursuit of God's kingdom very serious. They enter in at the strait gate and follow the narrow way which leads to life.

Chapter 2
SALVATION OF THE CHRISTIAN

Salvation of the Christian is about deliverance and freedom from the bondage of sin and eternal torment. The Christian is not a slave of sin anymore, and his soul yearns daily for God's kingdom. The system does not influence him anymore. The Christian experiences daily progressive sanctification as long as he remains in faith, abiding by the teachings of Christ. The Christian is a carrier of God's divine presence. True Christians manifest Christ's divine nature which includes His mercies, kindness, longsuffering, goodness and truth. The Christian is not a slave of sin but a free born; an heir of God's kingdom.

If any man be in Christ, he is a new creature: old things are passed away; behold all things are become new 2 Corinthians 5: 17.

The resurrection of Christ Jesus is the hope of our salvation, and the fear of the Lord is what actually keeps the Christian faith alive. Faith without the fear of the Lord and heaven at heart is dead and worthless. Many converts fear God and still fear other gods;

especially in Asia and in my African continent. Maybe they have forgotten the most High is a jealous God. Others fear God, but would not give up their lineage traditions and cultures which do not glorify the Almighty God. Many converts fear God, and still continue with human doctrines, religious formalities, forsaking the basic teachings of Christ which happens to be the only assurance of salvation. While some converts still uphold sound doctrine and would not compromise the Christian faith; many would not give up their holier than thou practices and self-righteous attitudes.

Isaiah 65: 5 which say, stand by thyself, come not near to me; for I am holier than thou. These are a smoke in my nose, a fire that burneth all the day.

WHAT DOES HOLIER THAN THOU PORTRAY?

Holier than thou practices and attitudes portray nothing, except profanity and self-righteousness. The holier than thou attitudes and practices were mostly found among the Pharisees, ancient Jewish scribes, and other ancient Jewish sects.

The Pharisee makes broad his garment, puts on sober attitudes in ceremonies yet devour widows, oppress orphans, and lives in the practice of secret sins. He pays tithes of all his possessions, he gives alms to the poor, offers assistance to the needy and also to the public. He is liberal and compassionate outwardly, but inwardly his heart is not right with God. Therefore, his giving and ceremonies are vain, except he repents of his hypocrisies and holier than thou behavior and conform to sound doctrine of Christ. The Pharisee is hypocritical in the inward. He uses religion to cover his ugly nature. Such a person cannot see the kingdom of God except his heart is renewed, and till his ways and actions become sanctify as God would have them be, he does not know God and His holiness.

Many converts think holiness is all about morality and quietness. Holiness is far beyond morality and gentleness. Morality alone does not amount to holiness of Christ Jesus. The problem with many converts these last days is over-zealousness, which leads to pride, arrogance and self-righteousness. Maybe they have forgotten that it was not by the work of our own righteousness that we are saved but by grace.

The moralist does not acknowledge the leadership of the Holy Spirit. He does not appreciate God's grace. He lives his life not according to the leading of the Holy Spirit and revelation of God's word which is the will of God, but by his own wisdom. Though he seems to be a good man among men; in the sight of men he is one who has never done anything wrong in his life. He treats his neighbor with respect and kindness. He thinks he is faultless, blameless, esteem by people because of his morality and no one ever doubted the purity of his manner, but he lacks true holiness. He does not bear false witness against his neighbor, he is honest as regard to morality and his temperament is what everyone could desire, yet he does not know God and His holiness. Holiness of our Lord Jesus Christ deals with the heart, thoughts and intents, aims and motives of men.

Morality does likewise but skims the surface and would not deliver the heart to God nor submit to the leading and yearnings of the Holy Spirit. Holiness of Christ transforms the inner man and requires that the heart should be set on God, submitting unto Him, fear Him and love Him without reservation. Many moralists are known for their good deeds but they are not in Christ. They profess Christianity but they are not saved.

The moralist believes in all principles of morality and manifests them outwardly with integrity of his own wisdom not through the Holy Spirit. He wouldn't submit to the yearnings and leading of the Holy Spirit because he trusts is in his own knowledge and wisdom.

The Christian can avoid the holier than thou behavior by conforming properly to basic doctrines of Christ Jesus, and also by submitting to the yearnings and leading of the Holy Spirit.

He will keep the feet of His saints, and the wicked shall be silent in darkness; for by strength shall no man prevail [1 Samuel 2:9]

If Christ had not risen from the dead, the Christian faith wouldn't be a saving faith, but because Christ Jesus is alive, we have hope and confidence that we are saved through the power of His resurrection. The Christian faith is about forgiveness, repentance, fear of the Lord, and heaven at heart. In today's church, many converts serve two masters, though God expects us to fear Him and serve Him alone in this world.

Matthew 6: 24 No man can serve two masters, for either he will hate the one and love the other, or else he will hold to the one and despise the other, ye cannot serve God and mammon.

Peter Mathias

JOHN 14: 2 In my father's house are many mansions; if it were not so I would have told you, I go to prepare a place for you.

The Christian faith is about heaven at heart and it strongly depicts the holiness of Christ Jesus. True converts believe heavenly treasures are far more precious than earthly values and vanities of this life. In trials and persecutions, and also in success, fame, and prosperity, salvation and eternal life remain the ultimate goal of genuine Christians because they understand life in this world is temporal not everlasting.

The Christian does not only prosper spiritually, mentally, healthfully but also financially and materially. Though, the Christian suffer many strange things in this world, reward of obedience awaits the faithful in Christ. It is the will of God that we prosper materially in this present material world, and above all, receive the crown of life on the last day as reward of obedience to sound doctrine of our Lord Jesus Christ.

However, the doctrine of Christ as the Bible presents it does not in any way encourage prodigality, materialism, and extravagance lifestyle. It does not esteem material mammon of this world and financial success above salvation and eternal life, but strongly emphases about heavenly treasures and everlasting life in Christ yet, it is the will of God that we prosper financially and materially in this world. Nevertheless, not God's will that we divert attention by focusing on earthly values and treasures, submitting unto mammon and forsake the ultimate purpose of salvation; which is about our heavenly treasures and eternal life in Christ Jesus.

MATTHEW 6: 21 For where your treasure is, there will your heart be also.

The basic doctrine of Christ requires that we set our affections on things above, not on values and treasures of this sinful world, but follow holiness in the fear of the Lord through Christ' teachings and inherit eternal life. Sound doctrine does not contradict holiness. How do I mean sound doctrine? I'm actually talking about the teachings of Christ which include: repentance, forgiveness, restitution, sobriety, pure heart, contentment, gratitude towards God, thanksgiving, selflessness, hospitality, faith, love, longsuffering, obedience to God, and looking unto Him [Christ] as author and finisher of our faith. True Christians are not materialistic; they are not greedy, and selfish, but sober, selfless, with all temperance through righteousness by faith in Christ Jesus. It is not a sin to be wealthy in this life, but wealth if not subdued and kept under control by faith is capable of enslaving the possessor.

The scripture clearly reveals that mammon is a spirit. Mammon happens to be the god of this present sinful world and it has strong influence over many lives in this world. Mammon is an enemy of righteousness. It actually kills, destroys and intoxicates people everywhere including many converts in today's church. Without money, survival in this modern world could be so unbearable, but submitting to the influence of mammon is more devastating and more painful.

The poor should be diligent and pray for financial blessings, and should not forget to keep mammon under feet when wealth comes. Converts whom God has given wealth should pray for grace that would enable them keep mammon under control, in other not to end up as slaves to their own wealth. Mammon is not a friend of any man. It is an enemy of righteousness. In this world, the influence of mammon is very strong.

Mammon is a prince among many converts in churches. Most modern converts glory in their wealth, and underrate the strategies of the prince of this world and wouldn't heed to the Lord's warning concerning serving two masters.

Wealth is not evil, but mammon, if not subdued and kept under control by faith may hinder the Christian from receiving the crown of life and eternal reward. This is the aspect many modern converts are not informed by their motivational speakers and prosperity preachers; though most converts already know this truth. To be sincere, poverty is not a good thing, it's horrible, however submitting to the influence of mammon is worst than poverty inherited.

The scripture is not against money and wealth, but the improper, and slavery attitude of men towards money and material possessions of this sinful world.

Peter Mathias

Chapter 3

GOD'S COVENANT WITH ABRAHAM

God's mercies brought us everlasting freedom. The Christian is liberated from the bondage of sin and eternal torment. Salvation which was earnestly expected by the prophets finally came the day Christ Jesus was born. God gave His only begotten Son to die for our sins. If not of the death, burial, and resurrection of Jesus, mankind would remain in bondage of sin forever. Our heavenly father by His infinite mercies intervened through Christ.

Salvation of the Christian is about eternal life in Christ Jesus. God started this work of salvation in the life of Abraham, Isaac, and Jacob, who later became the nation Israel. After the resurrection of Christ Jesus it was extended to all human races.

Looking at God's covenant to Abraham carefully, I could see salvation and mercy from God towards all of mankind. Sin which started with Adam was the problem of man for a very long period of time, and God allowed man to struggle with sin and conscience because Adam disobeyed Him and was not remorseful. After the fall; man still possess that moral sense that would enable him differentiate good and evil but was not able to overcome sin and satisfy conscience. The human race was left to struggle with sin and conscience for a very long time until the coming of the messiah.

God's covenant to Abraham is an everlasting covenant of mercy and salvation from the Almighty God. God played major role in the covenant making process by making all the promises leaving Abraham with little role to play. Abraham's part in the covenant making was only the circumcision of the flesh which he and his offspring from generation to generation must observe till the coming of the Messiah. According to scripture, this circumcision was to serve as an outward sign of the inward dedication to God.

The Abrahamic covenant was an unconditional covenant of grace and salvation from God. It was completely different from the conditional covenant of works God established with Israel of Moses days.

God's covenant to Abraham was without any binding agreement and was carried out only by God. Israel of Moses days had an agreement with God, and it was a binding agreement. God's covenant to ancient

Israel was not just a promise from God; it was a written agreement between Him and His people. The Almighty entered into an agreement with the Israelites. Unlike the Abrahamic covenant which was promise from God alone, the Jews had an agreement with Yahweh. God gave the people law and they promised to keep the ordinances of the Almighty God. God kept His own promises, but the people were not able to fulfill and keep their own part.

Exodus 24:7-8 And he took the book of the covenant, and read in the audience of the people and they said, all that the Lord had said we will do and be obedient. And Moses took the blood and sprinkled it on the people, and said, behold the blood of the covenant which the Lord had made with you concerning all these words.

At first, Moses read the testament before them and they all agreed to keep God's command. However, God kept His own promises but the people wouldn't keep their own and it attracted severe punishments and hostilities.

Jeremiah 34:18-20 And I will give the men that have transgressed my covenant, which have not performed the words of the covenant which they had made before me, when they cut the calf in twain and

passed between the parts thereof, the Princes of Judah and the Princes of Jerusalem, the Eunuchs, and the Priests, and all the people which passed between the parts of the calf; I will even give them into the hand of their enemies and into the hand of them that seek their lives and their dead bodies shall be for meat unto the fowls of the heaven, and the beasts of the earth.

God's unconditional covenant to Abraham reveals His immeasurable mercies and goodness. Through His conditional covenant to Israel of Moses days He demonstrated His righteousness and justice. His mercies endure forever though righteousness and justice is the foundation of His throne.

I have made a covenant with my chosen, I have sworn unto David my servant, thy seed will I establish forever, and build up thy throne to all generations. Psalm 89:3-4

But my mercy shall not depart away from him, as I took it from Saul, whom I put away before thee. And thy house and thy kingdom shall be established forever before thee: thy throne shall be established forever. 2 Samuel 7:15-16

The above scriptures were promises God made to David; it was not an agreement between Him and

David, but an unconditional covenant of mercy and salvation just like the Abrahamic covenant.

Jeremiah 31:31-32 Behold, the days come saith the LORD, that I will make a new covenant with the house of Israel, and with the house of Judah: Not according to the covenant that I made with their fathers in the day that I took them by hand and bring them out of the land of Egypt; which my covenant they brake, although I was a husband unto them, saith the LORD.

Jeremiah 31:31-32 is fulfilled the day Christ Jesus was born. As stated earlier, God started this work of salvation in the life of Abraham until He finally reached out to the whole world by giving His only begotten Son to die for our sins. Through the death, burial and resurrection of Jesus, the Christian is liberated from the bondage of sin by faith in Christ. The Holy Spirit renders help to true converts every day, and they experience daily progressive sanctifications as long as they continue in faith, abiding by truth with Heaven at heart.

Therefore if any man be in Christ, he is a new creature, old things are passed away behold all things are become new. 2Corinthians 5:17

Because of this progressive sanctification and help from the Holy Spirit, the Christian does not struggle with conscience anymore. The Christian depends on Christ's mercies and grace, His love and faithfulness through the fear of the Lord and a humble heart, in sobriety and by consistent gratitude towards God.

1 John 3: 19-21 And hereby we know that we are of the truth, and shall assure our heart before Him. For if our heart condemn us God is greater than our heart and knoweth all things. Beloved, if our heart condemn us not, then have we confidence toward God.

Christ Jesus lay down His life for our sins and He is alive forever interceding for the church. He is the author and finisher of our faith. He is our forerunner, redeemer and mediator of the new covenant. He took our place and died for our sins and wouldn't allow us to struggle with sin as long as we continue in faith looking up to Him as our helper by conforming to His basic doctrine. In the other words, if we forsake the pride of this life and submit to yearnings of the Spirit every day, we would receive grace that enables us keep going on daily basis and our salvation is sure. If we forsake His doctrine we are not looking up to Christ.

Chapter 4

WHAT EXACTLY IS HOLINESS?

Holiness of Christ is not religious formality, not intellectual ideas and precepts of men. It's not bondage but grace and liberty in Christ. Holiness is the beauty and glory of God. Holiness means perfection, purity, faultless and sinless. The pursuit of God's kingdom is about following holiness, though not without good works through faith in Christ Jesus.

Man lost this divine nature of God "holiness" in Eden; God restored it through Christ. Holiness is total separation from the world and total submission to God by faith through Christ. Holiness is not just abstinence from evil, worldliness and carnality. It is total abstinence from evil and sin, followed by good works through faith in Christ Jesus. Holiness is about the goodness of God Almighty. God is good, and out of the abundance of His goodness He created man so that man would resemble Him in goodness. In the other words, man was created to possess the character or the innate nature of the living God.

There are five strong attributes of holiness which the Christian must not fail to appreciate. These characteristics are similar to each other by their definitions, but we must study them word for word to enable us have clearer understanding concerning holiness of Christ. Conforming to these attributes practically means following peace with all men and holiness without which no man shall see the Lord.

Exodus 34:6 And the Lord passed by before him, and proclaimed the Lord God, merciful and gracious, longsuffering and abundant in goodness and truth.

The above scripture says, God is merciful, gracious, longsuffering, abundant in goodness and truth. Exodus34:6 actually unveil the character of God which is all about holiness. These attributes are: 1. mercy, 2. kindness, 3. longsuffering, 4. goodness, and 5. truth. I will begin with the word mercy or merciful which represents compassion and forgiveness because it came first in the above scripture.

1. MERCY:

> Our God is merciful and forgives people because He is holy. Holiness stirs up mercy and forgiveness from the inward. Forgiveness is an attribute of holiness not partial forgiveness, but genuine forgiveness triggered by the Spirit. A lot of converts profess holiness yet they lack the spirit of forgiveness. Converts who have

unforgiving hearts are yet to experience spiritual growth. I said so because unforgiving spirit is the absence of holiness. They yield to flesh more than they yield to God. One cannot be holy and lack the spirit of forgiveness. Holiness is mercy and compassion towards people. God is merciful and He forgives people their sins when they return to Him; most times before the people repent.

The story of the lost or prodigal son truly depicts the rebellious nature of mankind, the mercy of God, and His forgiveness.

Jesus said, a certain man had two sons, and the younger of them said to his father, father, give me the portion of goods that falleth to me. And he divided unto them his wealth. A couple of days after the younger son gathered all which belonged to him he journeyed to a far country and wasted his substance by prodigal lifestyle. When he had spent all there arose a great famine in that land, and he began to be in want.

Degraded by hardship he went into odd jobs for survival until he repented of his ways and returned to his father. The loving father saw him at distance and had compassion and ran and fell on his neck and kissed him and celebrated his return. That is how God forgives people out of the abundance of His mercies.

God is merciful and forgiving, not willing that any should perish. His desire is to see the restoration of that which was lost because He is merciful.

Luke 15:10 Likewise, I say unto you, there is joy in the presence of the Angels of God over one sinner that repenteth.

Luke 17:3 Take heed to yourselves, if your brother trespass against thee, rebuke him and if he repents forgive him.

Mercy is a very strong attribute of holiness. True Christians are merciful and forgiving because God is merciful and forgiving. Faith without mercy and compassion towards people is not genuine.

2. GRACIOUS

The scripture says that God is merciful and gracious. The word gracious simply means kindness or compassion. God is merciful and gracious in all His ways, thereby expecting the church to be gracious, because holiness of Christ involves sobriety and also compassion towards people.

Nehemiah 9:31 Nevertheless for thy great mercies thou did not utterly destroy them, nor forsake them, for thou art a gracious and merciful God

If one says he is holy or professes holiness yet the person is not gracious where is the holiness? The parable about the good Samaritan, is a short story of the Samaritan's kindness, and heartlessness of the holier than thou people.

Jesus said, a certain man went down from Jerusalem to Jericho and fell among thieves, they stripped him of his raiment and wounded him and departed, leaving him unconscious. By chance, there came down a certain priest that way and when he saw him he passed by on the other side. Likewise a Levite when he was at that place, came and looked on him, and passed by on the other side. But a certain Samaritan as he journeyed, came where he was, and when he saw him he had compassion on him, and went to him and bound up his wounds pouring in oil and wine and set him on his own beast and brought him to an inn and took care of him.

First the priest saw him and passed on the other side, and the Levite came and looked on him and also passed by on the other side. Now, the priest was a minister in the temple, a man of God to be precise while the Levite was an official who oversees the temple worship. But both were heartless in their behaviors yet they called on the name of God every day. Should we now say that these men were holy? Is holiness not mercy and compassion? I suppose holiness begins with the heart and thereby manifest outwardly as compassion. As a man thinks in his heart so is he in the outward and actions. We cannot give what we do not have. The holiness of Christ is a spirit. When the spirit comes and dwell in the inside, the convert would be gracious like Christ and His early apostles. Holiness stirs up compassion from the inward; it does not remain in the inside without reflecting outwardly.

3. LONG-SUFFERING:

Long-suffering means patience, endurance, forbearance, tolerance or slow to anger.

Psalm 103:8 The Lord is merciful and gracious, slow to anger and plenteous in mercy.

God by His long-suffering gives opportunity for repentance. Enduring and forbearing this world for ages because of His goodness. Holiness is forbearance and tolerance. Christ endured and suffered because of us, so He expects us to also love one another for salvation sake.

The parable of the wicked husbandmen portrays God's endurance and forbearance despite the sin of

Israel. Christ began to speak to the people in this parable: A certain man planted a vineyard, and let it forth to husbandmen (farmers) and went into a far country for a long time. And at the season he sent a servant to the husbandmen, that they should give him of the fruits of the vineyard, but the husbandmen beat him, and sent him way empty. Again, he sent another servant and they beat him also and entreated him shamefully and sent him away empty. And again, he sent a third and they wounded him also and cast him out. Then said the Lord of the vineyard, what shall I do: I will send my beloved son, it may be they will reverence him when they see him, but when the husbandmen saw him, they reasoned among themselves saying, this is the heir, come let us kill him that the inheritance may be ours. So they cast him out of the vineyard, and killed him. What therefore shall the Lord of the vineyard do unto them?

The owner of the vineyard sought to collect his share through his own servants but the husbandmen offered harsh resistance and turned down his request three times. Yet, he showed forbearance by sending his beloved son but they killed him. This was how God showed forbearance to the Jews for ages. That is to say that long-suffering emerges out of holiness. Holiness is not by power or by human efforts; it's the work of the Holy Spirit from within. Holiness produces forbearance and longsuffering.

4. GOODNESS:

Goodness is an attribute of holiness and this strongly emphasize about hatred towards evil. God hates evil and expect man to hate evil. Satan and his demons are evil. Worldliness is sin and sin is evil.

Amos 5:15 Hate the evil, and love the good, and establish judgment in the gate, it may be that the Lord God of host will be gracious unto the remnants of Joseph.

Good people hate evil. The fear of the Lord stirs up this hatred from the inward. Without the fear of God man wouldn't hate sin. The fear of the Lord propels goodness from within. Holiness is about the goodness of God. There is no difference between the goodness of God and holiness of Christ. Holiness of Christ is about the goodness of God. Job was an upright man, one that fear God and shunned evil (Job 1:1).

Good people hate sin; they are compassionate and diligent in well-doing by faith in Christ. Holiness is strong hatred towards worldliness, yet compassion towards people.

Matthew 19:17 And He said unto him why calleth thou me good there is none good but one that is God but if thou will enter into life keep the commandments.

There is none good but one does not deny His immeasurable goodness, but to let the young rich man know the seriousness of God's salvation and His abundance in goodness. God gave His only begotten son out of the abundance of his own goodness and love for humankind.

I strongly believe that the fear of God is the controlling principle of holiness. Holiness begins with the fear of the Lord from the inward, through total submission to Christ Jesus, and surfaces outwardly as God's goodness towards men.

There are two kinds of fear in existence and both have their effects in this life:

1. The fear of the Lord.
2. The fear of evil.

The fear of the Lord is conducive to health but, the fear of evil is unhealthy and does not in any way esteem holiness of Christ. The fear of the Lord provokes sound mind, inspirations, courage, boldness and strength. But the fear of evil produces depression and stirs up high blood pressure. The fear of the Lord stirs up joy from the inward, while the fear of uncertainty is nothing but complete despondent. The fear of the Lord is the good and healthy fear. Man is expected to fear God not evil.

Holiness begins with the fear of the Lord and strong hatred towards sin. A good man hates sin and shuns all the ways of this present sinful world. Holiness is strong hatred towards every form of worldliness and carnalities.

5. TRUTH

This fifth attribute of holiness refers to God reality, faithfulness and honesty. God is honest to man and to spirits.

Joshua 24: 14 Now therefore fear the Lord and serve Him in sincerity and in truth.

Joshua expressly warned Israel not to follow the ways of the Canaanites and other near east nations. God requested that Israel be sincere and honest in their relationship with Him. God hates worldliness and would not accept any form of carnality. As He called the Israelites out of Egypt and gave them ordinances through Moses, so He called the Church out of this world and gave the Church ordinances to follow through Christ. A true Church of God is an assembly or a group of baptized believers under the discipline of God's word (Gospel).

They are called to carry out the great commission, the administration of New Testament ordinances and the exercise of spiritual gifts. True Christians assemble for fellowship, reprove, instruction and worship. They carry out doctrine as it appears in the bible because they are separated from this world. God's word is true. We have seen the realities of His word with great signs of earthquakes, famine, wars and hypocrisies everywhere. The only prophecy which has not yet fulfilled is rapture.

Christ said He is coming back, and His testimony is true. The modern church should not forget letters from the island of Patmos to the seven churches in Asia; which reveals the Lord's warning, rebukes, reproves, and rewards from Him after this life (Revelation 2&3). Christ expects us to learn from these letters, and fear God, and follow holiness without which no man shall see God.

Peter Mathias

Chapter 5
THE WILL OF GOD

In these last days, many churches are very much reluctant in conforming to the basic doctrine of Christ Jesus, as if holiness is one big obstacle that can stop their successes in this world. They seem to have forgotten that Christ did not call His disciples unto the system of this world, but out of the system unto holiness. There are all kinds of holiness everywhere, yet holiness of Christ perfectly standout above all as the great light that shines in darkness; and the darkness comprehended it not [John 1:5].

Matthew 7 :21 Not everyone that saith unto me Lord, Lord, shall enter into the kingdom of heaven; but he that doeth the will of my father which is in heaven.

Matthew 7:21 is actually talking about God's desire, the purpose of church existence on earth and obedience to God's command.

What God require of us is obedience to His voice; that is by conforming to basic doctrine. Holiness of Christ is not a thing of this world, not human principle or religious practice but total conformity to the will of God and obedience to His command. This holiness is divine, yet a thing of growth from within when it involves the Christian. It may be in the heart just like the grain of mustard seed not yet developed; however, it may also be in the heart as a desire groaning and striving yet not completely realized, but as the Holy Spirit nurture it through the convert's total submission to the Spirit it grows to maturity. A regenerated heart or convert is an infant that need to grow unto maturity or purity.

Holiness is purity, and because it is perfection, no one who knows his own heart as a convert ever pretend to be perfectly conform to the will of God. The Christian experiences growth in holiness as he yield to yearnings and leading of the Spirit. Many converts do not simply understand holiness of Christ, yet they fast, pray, and call upon the name of the Lord every day. Others are not watchful concerning the day of the Lord or rapture which happens to be the earnest expectation of the saints. Could it be because they don't know what conformity to Christ means or are they still in the Dark Age when the Bible was available for only few people to read?

I cannot tell how, most end-time churches are actually getting ready for the second coming of Christ. But I wouldn't forget the scripture revealing that Christ will take those He finds waiting for Him in truth and in sincerity.

Lack of sound doctrine may deny many churches of these last days the kingdom of God. A lot of modern churches are not putting the primary teachings of Christ first and forward in their church doctrines. It is obvious most modern preachers hardly remember this secular world is Satan's world.

Proverbs 11:30 The fruit of the righteous is a tree of life; and he that winneth souls is wise.

Daniel 12:3 And they that be wise shall shine as the brightness of the firmament; and they that turn many to righteousness as the stars forever and ever.

Salvation and eternal life in Christ Jesus was the primary and regular discussions during the early church days. The apostles did not forsake the doctrine of righteousness by faith, forgiveness, repentance and restitution, hospitality, rapture, and eternal life for teachings that would enable them attain financial success in this world. They suffered adversity, yet salvation and eternal life remained their basic and regular discussions whenever they came together for fellowship and meetings during their days. By so doing, conforming to holiness of Christ was considered first above everything in their doctrine; and they were able to fulfill purpose in accord to God's will.

Today's church has different views about holiness; different teachings and doctrines everywhere. All kinds of denominations are what we have everywhere.

Christ predicted all these happenings; nevertheless God is not the author of this confusion. Many churches believe holiness is a thing of the heart alone which does not need to reflect through our dressings and wears no matter the offensive trendy styles. While some believe that holiness has a lot to do with the outward by appearing sober, and untidy. Others believe that holiness means isolated lifestyle; that is by religiously avoiding the company of other denominations and veiling every parts of the body except face, hands and feet.

In our modern days, a lot of converts have assumed salvation of the Christian to be comforts of this life only, thereby focusing on values and vanities of this life. If salvation is not about heavenly treasures, eternal life and freedom from bondage of sin, what then is salvation of the Christian all about? Is it food, drink, money and wealth? If the modern church uphold fundamental doctrine above every denominational doctrine, to exalt holiness considering how much the negative civilizations of this world is overtaking holiness in church, will God close the windows of heaven?

Will financial open doors and other blessings from God cease if we put the basic doctrine of Christ first and forward in our church doctrines? Most times, the reasons many modern preachers ignore the ultimate purpose of salvation and give much attention to things that are less important to the church could be so funny and unpleasant. Signs and wonders are now the unified theme of many church crusades everywhere without strong calls for repentance; yet the scripture says without holiness no man shall see the Lord.

LUKE 10:20 Notwithstanding, in this rejoice not, that the spirits are subject unto you; but rather rejoice, because your names are written in heaven.

*** Mark 8: 36 For what shall it profit a man, if he shall gain the whole world, and lose his own soul?***

Are we now going to forsake the substance and begin to pursue shadows? In Christianity, success is not about earthly achievements and making money. It is about making holy impacts and positive difference in people's live. Apostles of Christ did not forsake primary purpose "soul wining" for earthly achievements.

I believe God is faithful no matter the temptations of this present system which is attacking holiness in church. He expects His church to be faithful as well. Miracles, signs, and wonders are good, though these things do not guarantee the convert's eternal life. Material blessings are good, but it is not an assurance of salvation; it does not guarantee everlasting life. In our modern generation, many church goers acquire wealth but without heaven at heart. I mean without being renewed or regenerated in Christ.

Wherefore, gird up the loins of your mind, be sober, and hope to the end for the grace that is to be brought unto you at the revelation of Jesus Christ. As obedient children, not fashioning yourselves according to the former lusts in your ignorance: [1peter 1:13-14] To be sincere, this world does not have any good thing to offer to the church. Though, many preachers copy so much from the system. Every unholy idea church borrows from the world actually take virtue and value away from the church, and leaves the church spiritually empty. The world is very wretched; it cannot offer anyone things that will endure for ever because the glory is temporal yet, the Christian has so much to offer this corrupt world through Christ.

The intelligence of the enemy is far beyond the capacity of human intelligence. This is more reason the Christian needs the basic teachings of Christ and help of the Holy Spirit to overcome the strategies of Anti-Christ in today's church. As it is presently in our modern days, many churches are not different from business schools and the academia.

Church auditorium is a place for worship, not a class for business and financial studies but a temple for spiritual exaltation, edification of Christians and their preparation for the second coming of Christ.

Church structure is a holy temple and it should be seen as such. Christ did not redeem us by means of offering money to anyone; He redeemed the church by His own blood. He offered Himself as sacrificial lamb for the saving of all humankind. Values of this life cannot by any means represent the ultimate price Christ paid for our salvation.

Is church not a place where souls are edified for the second coming of Christ? Why is today's church now run after earthly treasures rather than seeking God's kingdom as the scripture reveals? Why are things that are secondary now coming first in the church? Reverse is the case in this present generation. Christ still expects us to seek His kingdom consistently and not relenting.

Bringing in business seminars and career seminars, into church auditoriums is not a holy idea. When the need of business seminars and other seminars which do not talk about Christ and salvation arise, let it be taken to classrooms. Church auditorium is not classroom, it is a sacred temple. It is not proper discussing hundred ways to manage business finance and two hundred ways to maintain financial success in the house of God, because such does not promote holiness among converts. Total conformity to God's will and obedience to His command is strait gate and narrow way which leads to life.

REVELATION 22: 12 And, behold, I come quickly; and my reward is with me, to give every man according as his work shall be.

Chapter 6
MATERIAL MAMMON

Mammon is the glory of this present material world. Mammon is god in this present sinful world and it rules over many lives mercilessly.

The Bible is not against money and wealth but that improper attitude of men towards money and material possessions of this corrupt world. Wealth is good when the Christian is able to subdue and keep the spirit of wealth under control. If it happens to be the other way round it will become so bad. Mammon belongs to this present sinful world; and it is a spirit. Nevertheless, God gives people wealth in this life and requires we obey Him not mammon.

For wisdom is a defense and money is a defense: but the Excellency of knowledge is, that wisdom giveth life to them that have it; Ecclesiastes 7: 12.

Wisdom is a defense and money is also a defense but the distinction here is life "eternal life". Wisdom gives life, money cannot give life. Wisdom keeps the wise going on the path of righteousness while money intoxicates the fool on the broad road that leads to destruction.

The Christian understands the ultimate purpose of salvation is not about comforts of this life, but eternal life in Christ Jesus. The Bible reveals the fear of the Lord is the beginning of knowledge; and to obey God is far better than keeping the treasures of this sinful world.

One fact most converts still fail to appreciate in these last days is about the strong influence of mammon in today's church. Maybe because many modern preachers still failed to appreciate that this world has a prince. However, the Christian can still overcome the prince of this world and his temptations by conforming daily to the teachings of Christ.

MATTHEW 4: 8 Again, the devil taketh him up into an exceeding high mountain, and showeth him all the glory of them; And saith unto him, All these things will I give thee, if thou wilt fall down and worship me.

Matthew 4: 8 is an example of how the prince of this world glories with mammon and also tempts the righteous. Mammon is an instrument by which he uses to keep many souls in bondage of sin and thereby destroys many lives. The influence of mammon in church alone this end time is devastating. The prodigal would not appreciate this fact. Though, these realities are far beyond what the ordinary eye can see.

Mammon is the pride of the enemy. It controls and intoxicates many converts in church, let alone outside the four walls of the church building. God requires we should not shift our attention from Him, the giver of wealth, to something else in this world.

The scripture is not against money and wealth as stated earlier, but that improper attitude of human enslavement towards material mammon of this sinful world. Constant concern over wealth and excessive regard for earthly values are capable of causing dangerous derail which may lead to serious spiritual pitfall. The scripture says, where your treasure is, there will your heart be also [Matthew 6:21].

Who knows the day of the Lord? The Bible says that no man knows the hour and the day of the Lord, not even the Angels of heaven [Matthew 24: 36].

Matthew 25: 1 says, the kingdom of heaven be likened unto ten virgins which took their lamps, and went forth to meet the bridegroom. Five of them were wise, and five were foolish. They that were foolish took their lamps, and took no oil with them: but the wise took oil in their vessels with their lamps.

In this parable the 10 virgins seem to represent the entire church of all ages. Beginning from the early church to today's church; not multiple brides. The one bride of Christ Jesus is the entire church.

The lamps refer to the lives or hearts which are either prepared or unprepared to receive the bridegroom. Salvation of the Christian is the state of having been saved from the bondage of sin and eternal torment. The Christian needs grace or help of the Holy Spirit to remain saved as he waits for the coming of the bridegroom.

Oil in this parable completely refers to that grace and mercy which prepares the Christian for the glorious wedding. This oil represents divine grace or help of the Holy Spirit which enables the Christian experience daily progressive sanctifications in Christ. If we look up to Christ as author and finisher of our faith by keeping His commandments, and yield daily to yearnings of the Holy Spirit, the oil that will sustain us and keep our lamps burning will not come short.

Philippians 2 :12 Wherefore, my beloved, as ye have always obeyed, not as in my present only but now much more in my absence , work out your own salvation with fear and trembling.

In Matthew 25:5 Jesus continued His parable: He says while the bridegroom tarried, they all slumbered and slept.

This simply implies the church dead silence in spirit and works during the Dark Age when original doctrine was forsaken and buried. Through early reformers such as Luther and other early protestant, original doctrine of Christ and that of His apostles was unveiled again. Today the church is sinking again into materialism, hypocrisies, and worldliness. Instead of Church making impact in the world, the system is the one now making so much impact in the church.

THE FALL OF MAN

There are questions surrounding the fall of man, and these questions come sometimes during Sunday school lessons in many local churches. Such as why did God create the serpent and allowed it to tempt man? Why did God allow the tree of the knowledge of good and evil to grow out of the ground in Eden? Now, looking at the whole thing, it appears a lot of converts put their blames on God each time they remember the fall of man.

I'm not going to answer any of these questions because I'm not God. But I understand the Almighty

God does not relate with people without putting ordinances and instructions in place. God set boundaries between the natural and supernatural. He put boundaries between the oceans and lands and instructed the fishes not to leave the waters, but inhabit the waters and live; and they obeyed. The fact still remains that God does not relate with His creatures without commands and instructions. Angels obey God; they take instructions from Him, and carry out responsibilities as instructed. Even animals hear God and obey His command without hesitation, but Adam whom God created in His image after His own likeness disobeyed his maker. Why?

And the Lord spake unto the fish, and it vomited out Jonah upon the dry land JONAH 2: 10.

1KINGS 13: 24 And when he was gone, a lion met him by the way, and slew him: and his carcase was cast in the way, and the ass stood by it, the lion also stood by the carcase .

The above scripture says, the lion also stood by the carcase. What stopped the lion from eating up the carcase or descend upon the ass? I think the lion did as instructed by God.

I would like to say that the serpent did not force Adam and his wife to eat the fruit. They ate it willingly against the will of God and disobeyed His command. The tree of the knowledge of good and evil was not the reason Adam and Eve fell, the fall of man was as a result of disobedience. Man was not made a robot. God created man a living being, and gave him sense of reasoning and ability to make choices in this life. There was no way God could have used mechanical device to stop Adam and Eve from eating the fruit; these people were not robots. God made them in His own image, after His own likeness and requires that man should obey His voice; though man disobeyed God. Adam had a unique relationship with God before the fall.

Peter Mathias

Chapter 7
ADAM'S AUTHORITY

God gave man authority over every creature on earth and that includes the serpent. [GENESIS 1: 26-28] The devil taking the form of a serpent to approached Eve simply means he submitted to the authority God gave man after creation. Adam lost that authority but Christ has restored more than what Adam lost in Eden. [Mark 16: 17-18]

MATTHEW 18: 18 Verily I say unto you, whatsoever ye shall bind on earth shall be bound in heaven; and whatsoever ye shall loose on earth shall be loose shall be loosed in heaven.

There is no authority on earth that is higher than what we have in [Matthew 18: 18]. The Christian faith is about authority in Christ. Authority over serpents and scorpions is what the Christian inherited from Christ Jesus. If Satan transform into serpents and scorpions to attack human; he is actually submitting to the authority God gave Adam and also the authority Christ gave to the Church.

Peter Mathias

As a deliverance pastor, I know demons most times take the form of serpents, owls, vultures, wolves, lions and other wild creatures to attack human spiritually. Satan can take the form of any beast to attack people. Christ has given the Christian authority over whatsoever the enemy may transform himself into. If the enemy chose to come as serpent; it is strong proof he is submitting to authority God gave man after creation. God said to Adam have dominion over the fish of the sea and over the fowl of the air, and over every living thing that moves upon the earth; which includes the serpent.

Several times during our church deliverance services I saw demons manifest out of people just like snakes and fish. Often I heard victims hiss, bring out their tongues like snakes, and even make moves on the floor like snakes and fishes in the water. Sometimes during hot prayer session and deliverance, some victims dance acrobatically. Most times these victims are violent before the demons finally leave them. Demons manifest out of people in different ways. Strange spirits come out of people by different means. For instance; through unusual sweating, vomiting, crying out very loud, uncontrollable sudden tears, body vibration or body shaking, unusual smiles, laughter and anger at same time etc.

This world is full of strange spirits, but authority is given to the Christian to trample upon all.

TIMES AND SEASONS

ECCLESIASTES 3: 1 To everything there is a season, and a time to every purpose under the heaven:

There is a season and a time to every purpose under heaven. As we cannot stop the winter, summer, fall and springs from coming, so we cannot stop certain troubles of this life from surfacing. God must glorify Himself. There are temptations God must allow to come in other to shame Satan and reduce him to nothing before everyone.

Romans 9: 17 for the scripture saith unto Pharaoh, even for this same purpose have I raised thee up, that I might show my power in thee, and that my name might be declared throughout all the earth.

In this life, the enemy has his own time and God has His own time. It is all about what God permits; and I see divine providence at work no matter the circumstances of this life. History did not take God unaware, so He knows what the future holds. The hour of temptation is the enemy's time, no man enjoys this hour, because it is horrible. However, the love of Christ produces endurance and grace these enable the Christian to keep going, despite the ugly seasons of this life. The Christian understands the hour of darkness is temporal, and does not last forever and the Christian is disciplined to wait upon God no matter what comes around.

But they that wait upon the Lord shall renew their strength; they shall mount up with wings as eagles; they shall run, and not be weary; and they shall walk and not faint. [Isaiah 40: 31].

GOD'S GLORY:

God's glory is far more than comforts and good things of this natural world. God's glory is beyond the beauty and splendor of this present material world. If you take a closer look at scripture intently, you will discover that God's glory is far beyond the treasures and luxuries of this life. Yet these things are the first to come to the mind of many modern converts whenever they think or remember God's glory (Matthew 6: 19-21). Material mammon and comforts of this present sinful world are nothing when compared with heavenly glory.

God's glory is inexplicable; far beyond human comprehension and it has nothing to do with this corrupt world and system. The glory of God commands attention both in the heavens and on earth and it produces riches on earth. Earthly values are inferior when compare with heavenly treasures. The scripture says, this present system and glory is reserved unto fire against judgment day and perdition of ungodly men [2 peter3: 7].

WHAT EXACTLY IS GOD'S GLORY?

The glory of God is about the beauty of His holiness. This comprises God's goodness, mercy, wisdom, longsuffering, honesty, riches, splendor, and power etc. God's glory is far beyond the comforts and good things of this natural life. Man was made to manifest this glory on earth. The scripture says God created man in His own image and after His own likeness.

Matthew 5:14 Ye are the light of the world. A city that is set on an hill cannot be hid.

The Christian is a symbol of God's glory on earth. The Christian carries God's glory in the inward thereby manifesting it outwardly on daily basis. The glory of God is what actually makes a convert real

Christian. The absence of God's glory in the life of a man amounts to a stony heart, unforgiving spirit, selfishness, greediness, pride, fear and everlasting shame at last. God's glory is eternal. In Christian life, it strongly involves grace and mercy from God. The Christian manifests God's glory as compassion, meekness, righteousness, and power through Christ Jesus. The glory of God radiates outwardly, though it begins with the inward. It begins with the heart through the spirit of the fear of the Lord and surfaces outwardly as exceptional wisdom, power, good understanding, sound health, sound mind, riches and every other blessing which the Christian inherited from Christ.

JOB 1: 1 Job was a perfect and an upright man, one that fear God and eschewed evil.

The first thing the scripture mentioned about Job was his uprightness and fear of God before the number of children and wealth. The number of his children did not come first neither did his wealth came first. His fear of God and uprightness came first. This simply means the fear of God and uprightness is what actually makes a convert real Christian not his possessions.

Chapter 8
BASIC KNOWLEGDE ABOUT CHRISTIAN FAITH

Hebrews 11:1 Now faith is the substance of things hoped for, the evidence of things not seen.

The above scripture stated the basic definition of the Christian faith. The substance of things hoped for and the evidence of the unseen realities. The most essential aspect of the Christian faith is the resurrection of Christ Jesus. He rose from the dead and His resurrection is our hope and courage. I will begin by talking about the substance of things hoped for, before I proceed to the evidence of the unseen realities.

SUBSTANCE OF THINGS HOPED FOR:

This refers to the fruits of the spirit and also the future hope of the church.

What are the things hoped for? Return of Christ, the glorification of the church, and eternal life in Christ. These are the future hope of the saints and the earnest expectation of the church. The substance of this future hope is fruit of the Spirit. Genuine converts bear fruits that befit repentance. The Christian faith involves the spirit of the fear of the Lord and also fruit of the Spirit. The fruits we bear through our obedience to God are the substance of things hoped for. God is at work in us through the Holy Spirit producing substance of things hoped. Saving faith emerges through total submission to Christ and it produces mercy, kindness, longsuffering, self-control, love, meekness, righteousness etc. Salvation of the Christian is not by human efforts; it is the work of Holy Spirit and it produces fruit that befits repentance among true converts.

Galatians 5:22-23 But the fruit of the spirit is love, joy, peace, longsuffering, gentleness, goodness, faith, meekness, temperance, against such there is no law.

Fruit of the Spirit is the visible substance of the Christian faith. The Christian by help of the Holy Spirit produces substance of things hoped for. This substance happens to be fruit of the Spirit. Beside fruit of the Spirit there is no substance, and if this substance is not found in a convert, the person's faith is vain and dead.

EVIDENCE OF THINGS NOT SEEN:

This refers to the unseen realities such as the presence of Holy Spirit on earth, the presence of angels, the forgiveness of sin, and Christ' present intercession in heaven. These are unseen realities and we have the evidence as Christians.

Romans 8:16 The spirit itself beareth witness with our spirit that we are the children of God.

The witness of the spirit is inward evidence of the unseen realities. While signs that follow the church and answers to prayers said according to God's will is outward evidence of things not seen. Evidence of the unseen realities is about God's mercies and grace which we enjoy every day.

Understanding the Christian faith can position the convert's heart towards the narrow way which leads to eternal life.

Hebrews 11:7 By faith Noah been warned of God of things not seen as yet, moved with fear prepared an ark to the saving of his house, by which he condemned the world, and become the heir of the righteousness which is by faith.

Peter Mathias

Noah had not seen rain, yet God told him to build an ark because of a coming flood and he obeyed. The time between Adam and the flood was one thousand seven hundred years. That is to say within these biblical years, there was no rain on earth. Noah was six hundred years old when the flood came. In the other words, from childhood to age five hundred and ninety nine Noah did not see rain yet he obeyed God and built the ark. The above scripture says Noah moved with fear. What fear? Noah, moved with the fear of the Lord prepared the ark. Through the fear of God, Noah demonstrated faith that pleased God. Without the fear of the Lord faith is dead. The fear of God is what actually keeps faith alive. One cannot have living faith without the fear of the Lord.

This world is full of noise with all kinds of distractions everywhere. The Christian is heaven conscious and spiritually minded. Distractions from different denominational doctrines and religious formalities alone are capable of manipulating modern converts. If the modern Christian fails to embrace sound doctrine as it appears in old King James Version (KJV), the wind of confusion may carry him away. Since the Bible was hand written centuries before the invention of the printing press, few copies were available. The Latin translation was the most common, but controlled by the catholic authority. Reformers such as Luther translated portions of the Latin Bible into German language. As Luther made the move to uncover the hidden Bible to his German people and others, some other early protestant from England were also compelled to do the same for England.

The King James Version of the Bible; I believe is the complete work of what Luther and other early protestant started. The Old Testament writings were in Hebrew and the New Testament in Greek before both were translated into Latin in the 5th century and the Latin translation became the official Roman Catholic Bible.

In 1545, the council of Trent met to reconsider doctrines and published some books which were accepted and considered canonical to counter the Luther reformation of the 16th century. The Luther movement was what led to the early German and English translation before the King James Authorized translation and Version. In our present generation, there are many Bible translations everywhere from different denominations. However I have decided to always keep the old King James translation closer to myself.

Peter Mathias

Chapter 9
LETTERS TO THE SEVEN CHURCHES

1. THE CHURCH IN EPHESUS

The church was commended because of their faith and perseverance through persecution. But was rebuked and urged to repent because they left their first love. They loved God at first; in the course of time the love reduced. This can happen when ulterior motives creep in among brethren. When the people are no longer heavenly conscious and spiritually minded, but believe in their human instincts more than the revelation of God's word, they will have less affection and little devotion to God. When converts allow self instincts and intellectual ideas to push away basic or fundamental doctrine, the love for God will reduce. When selfishness, greed, pride and materialism creep in among brethren, the love that the people have for God will disappear. Christ expects us to ignore all fleshly desires and yield to yearnings of the Spirit, conforming to basic doctrine daily by faith.

2. THE CHURCH IN SMYRNA

The Christians in Smyrna suffered much persecution. They suffered severe and intense persecution, and were reduced to poverty. They received no condemnation but were encouraged to endure persecution faithfully and wait for their reward. Their poverty did not compel them to engage themselves with business and career seminars in church auditorium. They were made to understand the faithfulness of God no matter the temptations of this life. Trials refine people and bring out their genuineness. God uses trials to nurture faith, so faith under attack is faith under construction. Persecution prepares the Christian for the crown of life. Faithful perseverance through trials shall be rewarded with the crown of life says our Lord Jesus Christ.

3. THE CHURCH IN PERGAMOS

The letter to the church in pergamos reveals the church compromised with paganism. The church was a state church with false leaders connected to the political system. Christ warned the entire church to repent of idolatry, immoralities, false teaching and follow sound doctrine.

This also refers to the paganisms of many today's churches. Many modern churches still have status which represents heavenly beings and portraits of one saint or the other in their church auditoriums; including the portrait of a famous actor who played the role Jesus of Nazareth in the movie Jesus of Nazareth, "Robert Powell". I don't think we need some sort of status and portraits of saints or heavenly beings in church. We have Christ our high priest in heaven. He is our mediator and forerunner. He intercedes for us at all time in heaven. We have God's word and we have the Holy Ghost here with us.

Exodus 20:4 Thou shall not make unto thee any graven image, or any likeness of anything that is heaven above, or that is in the earth beneath, or that is in the water under the earth.

Christ urged the Church to discipline herself by conforming to sound doctrine and should not tolerate false teachings and immorality within but follow holiness.

4. THE CHURCH IN THYATIRA

The church served God tirelessly but compromised with a false prophetess who refused to repent of her false doctrine and immorality. Christ referred the self proclaimed prophetess as Jezebel because she was leading the church into paganism and immorality by her false doctrine just as the Old Testament jezebel led ancient Israel into idolatry during the time of Ahab. The letter says judgment of God awaits her and her followers, because of their immoralities, and unrepentant behaviors.

5. THE CHURCH IN SARDIS

The church in Sardis received sound doctrine in the beginning. They heard and repented but slipped back into their old ways. Returning to their vomits without remorse, they became dead in spirit and works. They were few who did not regress to old ways. Christ urged the remnant to continue with original doctrine they received in the beginning. Warning those who went back to their old ways of the danger and judgment that lie ahead, He urged them to repent of their deadness and hypocrisy.

6. THE CHURCH IN PHILADELPHIA

Christ commended the Philadelphian church because they kept His word. The church followed the teachings of Christ and their reward shall be great. By this letter, Christ promised that He will rapture genuine converts out of this world before the world wide tribulation period begins. The time of temptation has not yet occurred. The worldwide tribulation is for the purpose of trying those whom the world and its system influence. The heathen and stiff neck converts shall suffer the world wide temptation. Christ promised to keep the faithful from the period of this great tribulation. The tribulation period is expected to take place after rapture.

The Philadelphian Church keeping the word simply means, they accepted original doctrine and followed holiness of Christ. The doctrine of Christ as the scripture presents it does not in any way encourage materialism, prodigality, and worldliness. It promotes sobriety, righteousness, and holiness. Sound doctrine does not encourage self esteem, self righteousness, and holier than thou behavior. It places much emphasis on total conformity to teachings of Christ Jesus.

7. THE CHURCH IN LAODICEA'S

The church is likened to lukewarm water, neither hot nor cold. Christ says He will spew them out except they repent of their lack of genuine faith. The church was famous for its wealth, but lacked spiritual value and virtue. Christ says they are spiritually poor and virtually worthless. This best described our current era fashionable and material churches that focus only on comforts of this life, giving little attention to the ultimate purpose of salvation which is about eternal life and heavenly treasures. These churches are not backsliding from their faith but they don't have genuine faith that can uphold basic doctrine and promote holiness of Christ.

TITUS 2:11-12 For the grace of God that bringeth salvation hath appeared to all men. Teaching us that denying ungodliness and worldly lusts we should live soberly, righteously, and godly, in this present world.

Chapter 10
THE CHRISTIAN CONDUCT AND DISCIPLINE

Salvation of the Christian begins with the inward, and surfaces outwardly. The beginning point of salvation is the heart. Salvation begins with the heart, thereby surfaces outwardly through good works, actions and sober conducts. Saving faith is what actually produces holiness from the heart. This true faith emerges as a result of total submission to sound doctrine of Christ Jesus, not religious formalities and human principles. Faith, whether weak, little, dead or alive appears outwardly. Faith is visible and very transparent no matter the type. Our outward conduct can also tell who we are in this world. The flesh has been an instrument of sin for a very long time in the hands of Satan. This is more reason good Christian conduct and self-discipline is very much important in the Christian race. The Bible says we should present our bodies living sacrifices to God.

Romans 12:1 I beseech you therefore brethren, by the mercies of God, that ye present your bodies living

sacrifices, holy and acceptable unto God which is your reasonable service.

The convert's body is a living sacrifice and also a means by which the holiness of God is reveal to this corrupt world. The ways of God is not the ways of this world. The ways of the world is worldliness. But the ways of God is righteousness and holiness. The flesh desire the ways of this world at all time. God has given us the privilege to make choices in this life. Nevertheless, what He requires of us is holy conduct and good Christian living as found in the Bible. Christ taught His disciples to resist all enticements, and influences of this sinful world, and follow holiness.

ALCOHOL:

Alcohol does not only intoxicate the mind, it speaks and deceives the drunk. Drunkenness is a spirit; a foul spirit from Abyss.

Alcoholic beverage is an intoxicating beverage made by the fermentation of sugar or sugar containing material. Alcoholic beverage is not natural, it is manmade. Drinking alcohol kills brain cells, damages liver, increases blood pressure and also affects blood sugar levels each time it is consumed. Alcoholic drinks such as liquors and beers, pose serious threats to human health. Many converts who love to consume alcohol justifies their drinking habits by referring to scriptures such as (John 2:7-11) and (1Timothy 5:23) If I may ask, did Christ give the people liquors, beers and alcoholic wine to drink?

Studies and research reveal the most common wine in Jesus days was grape wine. Grape juice could ferment and produces some alcohol when kept for a period of time. The worse and the good wine as stated in the Bible refer to the potent of both the worse and the good.

Christ did not give something different from fresh grape wine. He gave the sweetest and the freshest grape wine to the people by miracle. The water did not turn to beer, liquor, or any of the alcoholic beverages which we see these days. The water became fresh grape wine which was referred to as good wine. The governor of the feast called it good wine because it was fresh. There was no way the governor could have referred to an old fermented wine as good wine.

Fresh grape wine does not have one percent alcohol as content, except when it ferments, even at that, it will produce little percent of alcohol.

The good wine was fresh and it was referred to as good wine by the governor of the feast because it was fresh. Jesus knew the best drink to give people was fresh non-alcoholic drink; that was why He gave fresh wine, not fermented wine. Fresh grape wine does not intoxicate. No one should use Christ miracle at Cana to justify drinking beer, liquor, and other alcoholic beverages.

Some scholars and writers claim Jesus provided alcoholic wine, others say He provided beer to the people, yet can they produce any archeological evidence to back up their claim concerning ancient Israeli beer if there was any? Though it is not stated in scripture that if alcohol cross one's lips it is a sin; but it is obvious Jesus did not consume alcohol. His lifestyle is a perfect example of a true holy lifestyle.

I understand alcohol is drug; I also understand that a lot of medicines contain alcohol. A lot of medications such as tablets and syrups contain alcohol which serves for health purposes not sensual and for fleshly pleasures. Medicine restores good health and is not pleasurable. If it gives one pleasure then it is no longer medication but something else.

1Timothy 5:23 Drink no longer water, but use a little wine for thy stomach's sake and thine often infirmities.

Paul was not specific, though he couldn't have told Timothy to use strong wine because he knew the

Holy Spirit would not flow with alcoholic drink. Research reveals that grape wine was also the most common in the time of Paul and Timothy. Fresh grape wine is medicinal and non alcoholic. Fermented grape wine is also medicinal but with some alcohol about thirteen to fourteen percents. However, Paul instructed Timothy to use little wine because of his frequent stomach ailments. Timothy was not told to use beer or liquor, Paul said little wine. It could be alcoholic or non alcoholic. The purpose was because of stomach ailment and the instruction says use little which was not pleasurable.

Vineyards were very common in the ancient period near east region. What is vineyard? Vineyard is a grape plantation. Fresh grape wine does not intoxicate no matter how much it is consumed, but when fermented it can intoxicate if taken in excess. Fermentation in wine making is the process of turning fresh grape wine into an alcoholic grape wine. During fermentation, yeasts present transform sugar in the juice into ethanol and carbon dioxide. Alcohol is derived from ethane in the process of fermentation. Fermentation process allows yeasts to consume sugar turning the juice into an alcoholic wine. Ancient Israel produced both alcoholic and non alcoholic beverages and both were made from grape fruits.

And the LORD said unto Aaron, saying, do not drink wine nor strong drink, thou, nor thy sons with thee, (Leviticus 10:8-9). I believe the Christian is a royal priesthood, (1Peter 2:9).

Proverbs 20:1 Wine is a mocker, strong drink is raging, and who so ever is deceived thereby is not wise.

MODEST APPAREL:

Modest apparel is an example of holy conduct and good discipline. In this modern world, there are all kinds of trends everywhere that kick against holiness of Christ. The system has been corrupted by ungodly fashionable people with crazy trends.

1Timothy 2:9 In like manner also, that women adorn themselves in modest apparel with shamefacedness and sobriety, not braided hair, or gold, or pearls, or costly arrays.

The Apostle gave special attention to the female outward conduct and comportment because during early church the enemy attacked holiness through fashion. Though the female has a divinely implanted desire to have a good appearance, and Paul was not discouraging, that is because, neatness and tidiness is not a sin. Nevertheless, the woman is expected to avoid tight fitting dresses, sexy wears, and highly expensive dresses intending to impress people. He said the woman should adorn herself in modest apparel and this truly requires a sober and humble heart.

Shamefacedness and sobriety

Shamefacedness and sobriety in the above scripture refers to meekness, modesty, and broken spirit. These automatically cut off pride, arrogance, and silly behaviors.

Deuteronomy 22:5 The woman shall not wear that which pertaineth unto a man, neither shall a man put on a woman's garment; for all that do so are abomination unto the Lord.

This Old Testament commandment has stirred arguments among converts from different denominations. There are questions surrounding Deuteronomy 22:5 such as, should a woman wear trouser? Is it biblical to attribute trousers to men only? What stops the woman from wearing trouser since men of Old and New Testament days did not wear trousers but men are wearing it now?

Peter Mathias

The Bible through the history of Old and New Testament reveal that worshipers during this ancient period did not wear trousers, but were always on robe-like garments. David, Jeremiah, Ezekiel, and Daniel etc did not wear trousers. Christ and His disciples did not wear trousers.

Trousers were first invented around 500BC, simply because robes are uncomfortable to wear on horseback. Trousers were originally worn in the military and on horseback. Some historians stated that images of male and female horse riders wearing trousers can be found on ancient ceramics.

Trousers have been worn in Europe and Central Asia since ancient times. Initially, it was military dress during the Persian and the Greek kingdoms and empires. Those who wore trousers in battle had upper hand over those who wore robes. For this reason, civilizations all over the world adopted this form of dress to survive battle.

As trousers gain more popularity in the world many horse riders, male and female including athletes, began to wear trousers. Though, ancient trousers were loose fitting and big, modern trousers are tight fitting. When trousers were first invented, the trend was not tight fitting. What we have in our modern generation are tight fitting trousers everywhere.

In our present generation, we see tight-fitting trends specially designed for women and as they put on these dresses, it seductively brings out their natural physiques leaving them sexy and worldly.

In our civilized world there are different types of outfits everywhere. Many trends come out as tight-fitting wears, while others come out as well fitting wears. Outfit that appears well fitting on Christian woman is not bad, but tight-fitting does not befit repentance. I'm not going to say if a woman wear trouser that it is sin, because I can't find that literary written in the Bible. I'm aware many modern women wear trousers for different reasons. However, I would like to share my thoughts concerning this controversial issue, but from God's word.

I know we are different people from different cultures and backgrounds, and we think and also appreciate things differently due to church denominational doctrines, but we have God's word and it is our principal teacher.

Isaiah 3:16-26 reveals the strong hatred God has towards every form of carnality and worldliness.

Peter Mathias

ISAIAH 3:16-17 Moreover the LORD saith, because the daughters of Zion are haughty, and walk with stretched forth necks and wanton eyes, walking, and mincing as they go, and making a tinkling with their feet:

Therefore the LORD will smite with a scab the crown of the head of the daughters of Zion, and the LORD will discover their secret parts.

The biggest problem which associates with today's church is worldliness. The system has creep in so deeply into the church to the extent many preachers don't have any choice, but welcome whatever that comes around.

It is highly disappointing because most modern preachers still do not see the extent negative civilizations of this sinful world has penetrated modern Christianity. I strongly believe God is at work no matter the manipulations of anti-Christ in today's church.

ISAIAH 62:1 For Zion's sake will I not hold my peace, and for Jerusalem's sake I will not rest, until the righteousness thereof go forth as brightness, and the salvation thereof as a lamp that burneth.

As a deliverance pastor and a preacher of holiness, I understand tight-fitting trends and other trendy-styles that expose women breasts everywhere came into existence through unholy ideas which do not esteem femininity. In our modern world, most Christian women don't only wear tight-fitting trends to church; they also wear outfits that expose part of their breasts. I would like to say that this modern fashion style and unholy civilization do not do the church any good, it steals virtue and honor from the womanhood.

It is appropriate for a man to wear trouser to church. I don't think it is suitable for a woman to wear trouser to church no matter how feminized it may appear, except otherwise. Reasons: when a man wear trouser, he does not only appear masculine but decent and a man putting on trouser to church is not a stumbling block to decencies and holiness in church. Please, let's be spiritually minded here.

Masculine trousers do not wage war against holiness in church feminized trousers do most times; maybe because of their sexy pattern and design. When a woman puts on trouser to church she may appear feminine, yet not decent. Modern feminized trousers are mostly tight fitting, sexy, and seductive. Though, trousers were first invented for easy movement, flexibility, and comfort.

Sexy trends are unholy ideas from the world. Many modern preachers and converts hardly remember that this present material world is the enemy's world; so they welcome every fashion styles that come their way without hesitation. I know most Christian women wear trousers simply because they want to look modern and smart. While others wear trousers because of their jobs; many still wear trousers because they want to look sexy everywhere they go.

However, I appeal modern preachers should strive and avoid unfavorable civilizations of this world which attempts to promote worldliness in church. I say this because this present material world is Satan's world. The Christian is separated from the world and called to be holy unto God. When change occurs in the inside, the world around us changes as well, and this includes our outward conducts and comportments.

ROMANS 8:6 For to be carnally minded is death: but to be spiritually minded is life and peace.
JOHN 17:16 They are not of the world, even as I am not of the world.

VEIL ON WOMAN'S HEAD:

1Corinthians 11:15 But if a woman has long hair it is a glory to her, for her hair is given for covering.

The Bible says if a woman has long hair it is a glory to her. It is common to see young women who lack long hair wish they have it. The scripture says the female long hair is a glory to her. The word "glory" in the above scripture stands for natural beauty. The female long natural hair is for her own beauty.

For covering refers to the long natural hair given to her to cover her insensitive shyness. As it was during ancient Israel; ancient Israeli women valued long hair and kept it to their own glory. The Apostle was not saying the woman's long hair can also represent veil on her head in God's presence.

If a woman veils her head before coming to God in prayers or worship, it is a sign of respect to Angels. The early church kept this tradition, and I believe it is a decent comportment. If observe by the modern church it is a good tradition. [1Corinthians 11:10]

1CORINTHIANS 11:5 But every woman that prayeth or prophesieth with her head uncovered dishonoreth her head: for that is even all one as if she were shaven.

Peter Mathias

Chapter 11
EARRINGS:

Let me begin by saying that no one was born with ears divinely pierced open for rings. Piercing originated from ancient near east among the idolatrous men and women of the region. It was the custom of the ancient near east idolaters and idolatresses to pierce part of their flesh for rings and chains in accord with tradition and culture.

The Bible clearly reveals that earring and other ornaments were considered idols and strange gods by Jacob. Ornaments wouldn't allow the Israelites give God their full spiritual attention and concentrations after the exodus. This happened because they valued ornaments and place it above God in their lives.

Genesis 35: 4 And they gave unto Jacob all the strange gods which were in their hands, and all their earrings which were in their ears, and Jacob hid them under the oak which was by Shechem.

In the course of preparing for worship; Jacob took all earrings from his people and hid under the oak. This was because he knew ornaments would not allow them give God their full spiritual concentrations. Israel of Moses days went out of Egypt with so much gold earrings, nose rings, necklaces and everything made with pure gold.

Exodus 12: 35 And the children of Israel did according the word of Moses, and borrowed of the Egyptians jewels of gold, jewels of silver, and raiment.

The purpose of all these jewels of gold and jewels of silver was not for their own adornment, but for God's tabernacle. Though, it was misused by Aaron but the remnants were later used for the purpose by Moses.

Exodus 35: 22 And they came both men and women as many as were willing hearted, and brought bracelets, and earrings, and rings and tablets all jewels of gold and every man that offered, offered an offering of gold unto the Lord.

The scripture says all the offerings of gold were used to construct and furnished the tabernacle. Moses did not permit the people to wear earrings again because such practice frustrated the worship God required of His people. During Moses days, ornaments caused huge distractions and frustration in the wilderness. It kept many Jews in bondage of their own flesh, which attracted severe punishment to the people. Piercing the flesh for rings was a common traditional ritual among ancient Egyptians, Canaanites, and other pagan kingdoms of that time. What is the message here?

Civilizations and cultures of this world that wouldn't allow the Christian yield effectively to God, and follow holiness of Christ are not worth retaining. That is the message.

Exodus 33:5-6 For the Lord had said unto Moses, say unto the children of Israel, ye are a stiff-necked people; I will come up into the midst of thee in a moment and consume thee, therefore now put off thy ornaments from thee, that I may know what to do unto thee. And the children of Israel stripped themselves of the ornaments by mount Horeb.

During Gideon time, God gave His people victory over the Midianites who were also known as Ishmaelites; and they ran and left all their golden earrings behind. The Israelites invaded their camps and went away with all the golden earrings, but Gideon collected everything from the people and used all for ephod. Just as Moses did not also allow his own followers to wear earrings.

Peter Mathias

Judges 8:24 And Gideon said unto them, I will desire a request of you, that ye would give me every man the earrings of his prey. For they had golden earrings because they were Ishmaelites.

THE KINGDOM OF BEAUTY:

The kingdom of beauty warned a young lady not to attend prayer vigil in our Church, though she disobeyed and came for the vigil. As the worship was on-going, the enemies struck and she slumped and fainted. When God revived her some minute interval, she confessed the kingdom of beauty warned her to stay home that night but she refused. This was how I came to know about the kingdom of beauty.

I wouldn't also forget how a demon spoke from same person during one of our church deliverance programs and said her name was Cynthia from the Indian Ocean. She said in their kingdom they produce beauty colorants such as lipsticks, eyeshades etc. I know this may be hard to believe, but it was what I actually encountered during deliverance work; and my testimony is true.

I'm not taking anything here personal because I know quite well that this life is full of mysteries. But it will be unwise for me to condone or accept whatsoever demons passionately love.

I have asked myself why demons so much love some names people cherish in this world; and I was left without answer because I don't have any answer to such question. However, I'm not sentimental about names demons love and names they don't love. I understand it is more of spiritual rather than physical, though this may not go well with many modern converts. Nevertheless, if convert who has a name that is faulty, forsake such name for a better name I don't think there is any problem with that. I speak as a deliverance pastor.

Through my encounters so far during deliverance works; I got to know that some names many parents love to give girl child in this world have strong spiritual significant connecting to deities. Example of such names is Diana.

ACTS 19:34-35 But when they knew that he was a Jew, all with one voice about the space of two hours cried out, great is Diana of the Ephesians. And when the town clerk had appeased the people, he said, ye men of Ephesus, what man is there that knoweth not how the city of the Ephesians is a worshiper of the

great goddess Diana, and of the image which fell from Jupiter.

BEAUTY COLORANTS:

Beauty-colorants refer to substances apply to the skin for beauty sake. During ancient near east period; painting served as a form of ritual which pagans must observe before worships or feasts. Though, many harlots were also known for colorants they apply on their skin especially on their faces; painting originated from paganism.

Applying colorants on skin was part of tradition of the ancient near east prostitutes and pagans. The idea of painting and piercing the flesh for beauty sake started in the ancient near east region among pagans.

2Kings 9:30 And when Jehu was come to Jezebel, Jezebel heard of it and she painted her face and tied head and looked out at a window.

Ezekiel 23:40 And furthermore, that ye have sent for men to come from far, unto whom a messenger was sent, and lo, they come, for whom thou didst wash thy self, painted thy eyes, and deckedst thy self with ornaments.

During ancient Israel painting was envisioned as carnality, thereby considered offensive by ancient Israeli prophets and Jewish rabbis.

God expects His own people to avoid cosmetics that attempts to change their natural skin appearance. God created everyone perfect and no one can improve God's hand work. The Christian is expected to avoid every man made artifices which opposes holiness of God and promote worldliness.

I'm not by any means saying if one wear makeup the person is a prostitute, and I'm not saying all cosmetics are offensive. But artifices such as artificial eyeliners, artificial eyelashes, artificial nails, and beauty colorants lack reverence for God. God doesn't want His own people to wear all these things, paint or change their natural skin appearance but use good cosmetics to maintain it.

Peter Mathias

Chapter 12
SOUND DOCTRINE

I believe God raises church leaders to guide brethren in accord to basic doctrine of Christ. Pastors are not expected to bring in intellectual ideas that may oppose God's will.

God has His own role in church, and pastors have their own responsibilities given to them by God. Man cannot leave his own role to hijack God's role. The work of sanctification and justification is God's duty in Church. Pastors are called to lead with total submission to God. Pastors are not called to make holy or condemn any man. The Christian grow in sanctification by faith in Christ. Salvation of the Christian is not the work of men but God's work.

True Christians uphold the fundamental doctrine of Christ Jesus above every church denominational doctrine. One can still know true followers of Christ by their fruit. Fruit which we bring forth refers not only to actions of our lives, but doctrine we proclaim.

During early church the apostles taught converts to live soberly, righteously, resisting lust, greed, and pride of this life. The people were disciplined to exercise self-control, have contentment at all time, and not passionate about vanities of this life.

REPENTANCE:

What is repentance?

Repentance is remorse, a penitent, sorrowful heart on account of sin; a feeling of regret for doing wrong. Repentance is not perfection. But, there are evidences that accompany genuine repentance.

One of the strongest act of faith, which is a strong proof of genuine repentance is restitution. Genuine repentance leads to a desire to correct wrongs.

Luke 19:8 And Zaccheus stood, and said unto the Lord, behold Lord the half of goods I give to the poor, and if I have taken anything from any man by false accusation, I restore him four fold.

Zaccheus repented and we could see the evidence of his repentance in his immediate decision to make restitution. The proof of his repentance and conversion was his resolve to make restitution. When one becomes a Christian, the person would have an inborn desire to correct wrong. Restitution is not about compensating only those we have wronged. It is about our unreserved compassion towards people generally for salvation sake.

Restitution is not a requirement for salvation, but it is an evidence of genuine repentance. There are sins for which there is no adequate restitution. In such instance, the convert is expected to make some form of restitution that demonstrates true repentance or penitence, but at the same time does not need to feel bad about the inability to make full restitution. Making restitution does not mean we are paying for our sins or paying for our salvation but it is an act of faith which demonstrates sound repentance and gratitude towards God for His mercies and forgiveness. Restitution is expected from the Christian, but the Christian does not expect restitution from anyone. Making restitution to people we have done injustice to before conversion is necessary because it will enable the convert to win the people's forgiveness. Literally, restitution is an act of returning something that has been stolen or compensating for the theft of or damage to properties.

Titus 3: 5 Not by works of righteousness which we have done, but according to his mercy he saved us, by the washing of regeneration, and renewing of the Holy Ghost.

Peter Mathias

Salvation is about mercy from God towards humanity. However, no one can partake of it by trying to obey God's word literally or by human effort. It is the work of the Holy Spirit and it begins with new heart from God. Christ didn't come for the righteous. He came for sinners to repent and be free from the bondage of sin. Though the holier than thou would not appreciate this fact because he strives to keep God's word literally; and considers himself the best among converts. He believes a mere hand shake with sinners can defile the Christian. The faith of the holier than thou portray nothing but pride which shall amount to judgment.

Chapter 13
BORN AGAIN

What does it mean to be born again? To be born again means to receive a new heart from God. New heart from God is about power to live a holy life.

Psalm 51:10 create in me a clean heart, oh God and renew a right spirit within me.

David requested for a new heart which is about power to live a holy life. The same is applicable when one gives his life to Christ. Clean heart means a new heart from God. When one repents genuinely and gives his life to Christ the person automatically receives a new heart from God. That is what it means to be born again. Genuine repentance followed by sincere confession, attracts power that will enable one live a new life in Christ. Christianity is more than a mere religion; it is about new heart from God, power to live a new life in Christ.

John 1:12 But as many as received Him, to them gave he power to become the sons of God

The scripture reveals the Christian has power to live a holy life through Christ. Grace is given to the

Christian by God to ignore fleshly desires, and yield to yearnings of the Holy Spirit. Power for holy life style comes from God. This power is power of regeneration and it comes from God.

Roman 8:1 There is therefore now no condemnation to them which in Christ Jesus, who work not after the flesh but after the spirit.

When one receives a new heart from God, I mean heart that forsakes the ways of this sinful world and follow holiness of Christ then the person is born again. Though man lost that innate nature of God but Christ restored it on the day of His resurrection. The resurrection of Christ Jesus is complete victory over sin and its bondage. The power of resurrection enables people who did not know God to know Him through Christ, and they receive grace to follow holiness of Christ.

1corinthian 15:17 And if Christ be not raised your faith is vain, ye are yet in your sin.

Christ came from heaven to earth to save us from bondage of sin. There is no deliverance that is greater than one receiving a new heart from God. As a result of new birth in Christ, the Christian received grace which enables him to seek God's kingdom and His righteousness. The Christian is regenerated and transformed as a result of grace and new heart from God.

The Christian understands the ultimate purpose of salvation is not about earthly achievements, but eternal life in Christ Jesus. Though, apart from this basic grace of new heart from God; the Christian also need everyday grace from God that will enable him overcome daily strategies of Satan. We know old things are passed away but we are not ignorant of devices of the devil. New life in Christ does not change the fact that the Christian is engaged in everyday spiritual warfare. (Ephesians 6:12).

Peter Mathias

Chapter 14
ASSURANCE OF SALVATION

The Bible clearly teaches that it is possible to know whether one is saved or unsaved. The witness of the Spirit is assurance of salvation. If one is truly saved, the Holy Spirit would always reveal the person's spiritual status beforehand.

2Timothy 4:7 I have fought a good fight, I have finished my course, I have kept the faith.

Paul's confidence was not based on emotional feelings or human instinctive feelings, but on proves. Salvation of the Christian is not about feelings, but about proves in accord with God's word. Total submission to Christ and His teachings is assurance of salvation.

A genuinely saved person is one who conforms to sound doctrine of Christ Jesus. The Christian continually lives in obedience to the revealed will of God as the normal way of life.

There are four strong proves that can help the Christian know he is saved:

1. **Obedience to God**

The assurance of salvation lies in obedience to the revealed will of God. When one realizes this truth, then he or she is ready for eternal life. The only way one can successfully submit to God's will is by conforming to fundamental doctrine of Christ Jesus, and submitting daily to leading of the Holy Spirit. After repentance and conversion, God's word requires we present our mortal bodies living sacrifices, holy and acceptable to God. (Romans 12: 1).

The convert's body is temple of God from the day of new birth in Christ, and should be seen as such.

The believer's body is not for tattoo, incisions, piercing, and immoralities. Though, these things are desires of the flesh and pride of this life. But God has given the Christian power to ignore fleshly desires. The flesh and the spirit have desires and yearnings that are contrary to each other but the Christian yields daily to yearnings of the Spirit.

2. Gratitude towards God

The scripture says give thanks to God always for all things.
[Ephesians 5: 20]

True Christians are thankful to God no matter the circumstances and temptations of this life.

Thankfulness and gratitude to God was tradition the early church inherited from Christ and His apostles. The Holy Spirit enable's the Christian to be grateful to God in every circumstance. The Christian is not stingy, but liberal because of Christ mercies and suffering of the cross.

Giving for the propagation of the gospel is another means of expressing gratitude to God for His mercies and forgiveness. Heart of gratitude towards God is among proves that enables the Christian knows he is saved. The unthankful will not by any means see the kingdom of God. Thankfulness and gratitude to God is assurance of salvation.

3. **The spirit of intercession**

What is intercession?

Intercession is about justice, truth, mercy, righteousness and prayers. It is an act of mediating, intervening or standing in gap. [Isaiah 59: 16] Intercession was part of the tradition of the early church. The Christian is disciplined to intercede for brethren and also for sinners. The Christian is an intercessor who pleads to God on behalf of people. Intercession is about selflessness and compassion towards people no matter their races. Just like Abraham who expressed concern for the people of

Sodom and Gomorrah, the Christian is compassionate, sober, and selfless in all his ways.

The spirit of Intercession is concern not for oneself but for others without any ulterior motive. The Christian expresses concern for people's welfare and also for their salvation. The spirit of intercession is also assurance of salvation.

4. Charity

The early church was also disciplined to remember Golgotha and love one another with heart of gratitude towards God for His mercies and forgiveness. Agape is God's kind of love; it is an attitude of kindness towards people. The Holy Spirit stirs this love of God from the inward and the Christian manifests it as led by the Spirit. Christ suffered for all and what He expects from us in return is not pride and selfishness, but humility and love towards one another.

John 13:34 A new commandment I give unto you that ye love one another as I have loved you that ye also love one another.

Christ expects us to reciprocate His love through good works and compassion towards people. The Christian appreciates the suffering of the cross and expresses gratitude to God by conforming to His revealed will. True Christians are sober and loving, but they don't submit to influence of this world, charity does not push holiness of God aside. Agape truly depicts holiness of Christ and it is an assurance of salvation (1Peter 4:8).

Peter Mathias

Chapter 15
LET THE WOMAN LEARN IN SILENCE

1 Timothy 2: 11-12 Let the woman learn in silence with all subjection. But I suffer not a woman to teach, nor to usurp authority over the man but to be in silence.

1 CORINTHIANS 14: 34-35 Let your women keep silence in the churches, for it is not permitted unto them to speak, but they are commanded to be under obedience, as also saith the law. And if they will learn anything let them ask their husbands at home, for it is a shame for woman to speak in the church.

What message are these scriptures passing across to the church? And what was the message to early Christian women?

Before we go into the message, let's first look at both scriptures literally and also traditionally. If we take both scriptures word for word it means women should not speak in the church. They should not say a word in church let alone prophesying, preaching, teaching, praying or talk in church. Not only that, women whether young or old should learn in silence with subjection to all men.

The above scriptures say if women will learn anything let them ask their husbands at home, for it is a shame for woman to speak in the church.

The apostle said that it is a shame for woman to speak in church. Now, looking at the whole thing literally, this command did not only disqualify women from preaching in church it also forbid them from talking in church. Could that be the message from the apostle?

Paul actually admonished early church women to forsake pride, arrogance, and every irritated attitude that may stir up quarrel and silly arguments in church. The early Christian women were taught to be meek and sober; not quarrelsome and contentious, but submitting to their husbands at home.

Let your women keep silence in the churches, was a command which upholds sobriety and meekness among early church women. Paul was not saying the woman wouldn't preach or teach in church. If God choose to pass His message across to church through a woman, can anyone stop Him? Was Deborah not a woman? [Judges 4:4]

***1 CORINTHIANS 11:4-5** Every man praying or prophesying having his head covered, dishonoureth his head. But every woman that prayeth or prophesieth with her head uncovered dishonoureth her head: for that is even all one as if she were shaven.*

The scripture says both men and women did prophesy in the church and Paul did not discourage that, instead he gave ordinances that would help them conduct themselves properly in God's presence.

Joel 2:28 reveals, both sons and daughters shall prophesy. It was a promise to ancient Israel before the church was born. To prophesy means to speak with divine inspiration and it involves teaching and preaching. The Spirit of God spoke expressly through Joel that both sons and daughters shall prophesy in the congregation of saints. Not sons only, but sons and daughters shall prophesy.

Nevertheless, the apostle used (1Timothy 2:12) to let the woman understand the authority that exists above her, still under Christ. The head of the woman is the man and the head of every man is Christ. The authority God kept above the woman is her husband still under Christ. Therefore, the woman is not permitted to exercise authority over the man except delegated by God as calling which is on spiritual basis and not lordship over the man.

Christ is the head of the church and He called both the man and the woman into the ministry. The scripture says entreat older women as mothers and younger women as sisters with all purity.

Ephesians 5:21 Submitting yourselves one to another in the fear of God.

Ephesians 5:21 is about mutual submission and it strongly depicts Agape. The Christian is a laborer called to serve in the Lord's vineyard. Submitting one to another in the fear of God is about respecting and serving each other in the fear of God. The church comprises servant leaders, servant fathers, servant mothers, servant husbands, servant wives, servant brothers, servant sisters and children.

The scripture says, as the church is subject to Christ, so let wives be to their own husbands in everything. Christ is equal to God the father and still subject to Him. A Christian wife sees her own husband not only as a spouse, but as one having the authority to lead in the marriage.

1 Peter 3 : 6 Even as Sara obeyed Abraham, calling him Lord, whose daughters ye are, as long as ye do well, and are not afraid, with any amazement.

Husbands are to love their wives, while wives are expected to reverence their own husbands. Love is kindness, honesty, and respect. A husband is expected to love his own wife in accord with God's word. For a husband to become a Christ like leader he must be willing to first make himself into a servant by avoiding the pleasure and pride attached to holding headship in marriage and submit to God. And wife must also strive to avoid the temptation of toppling her own husband and overturning her marriage against the will of God.

Adam was not deceived by the serpent, Eve misled Adam. Why the serpent avoided Adam and went to Eve is a question which I have not gotten a satisfiable answer for it. Could it be because she was the weaker vessel, or because she loved flashy things?

Genesis 2:24 Therefore shall a man leave his father and his mother, and shall cleave unto his wife, and they shall be one flesh.

God initiated marriage between the first man and woman in Eden. He created Adam first, then Eve and brought Eve to Adam. If spouse fails to leave and cleave, problem may emerge in the marriage. Leaving your previous family means you understand that your marriage creates a new family which is a higher priority than the previous one. Though, leaving your parents does not mean forsaking them but if spouse fail to leave and cleave, the ultimate purpose of marriage will not be realized.

Good marital intimacy and one flesh. And they shall be one flesh. This means love that wouldn't involve any third party except God who introduced marriage to human. We do not quit when things are not going well. We seek God's counsel always in His word, learning every day, forgiving each other, accepting God's counsel, and praying things through.

Chapter 16
A HUSBAND LEADER

Leadership role in marital home is a husband's role in marriage. The bible stated it very clear that a husband must take the lead in his marital home. The scripture says, wives should submit to their own husbands as unto the Lord. [Ephesians 5:22-24]

The word head means responsible one or one having the authority to lead. The apostle used the example of Christ as head over the church so that a husband would compare his actions with that of Christ's and emulate him. A husband leader looks up to Christ as ultimate role model of true leadership. A husband leader strives to model Christ in leadership.

Though many husbands have simply refused to lead, while others do not understand how they should lead, many still fail to realize that the responsibility is a husband's role in marriage. Lack of husband's leadership in marital home creates serious marital problems and other series of problems in marriage.

The problem facing many marriages and homes today is lack of husband's leadership. It is the will of

God that the man lead while the woman assist and encourages him to be more Christ like in his leadership.

When a husband fails to lead, he becomes a rebel that is not submitting to God's will. That is by failing to accept his leadership role. Many husbands are just too lazy and would rather leave their leadership role in their homes to their wives. Others easily give up due to their wives constant verbal attacks that remind them of their weaknesses and imperfections. A whole lot of husbands are manipulated by their wives to forsake their leadership obligations. This can happen through the woman's regular intense tears, constant criticisms, persistent verbal abuse, and reminding the man about his poor decisions in the past.

The reason many modern husbands still fail to accept their leadership role is negative media influence. Though many married men did not see lineage leadership example in their previous families as they grew up. Nevertheless, a husband must first believe that God called him to lead and must be ready to lead in love and affection towards his own family. Love is not weakness but boldness, courage and selflessness. Love is not laziness love accepts responsibility and does not fail to deliver. [2Timothy 1:7]

Christ while on earth was strong, bold, and gentle as the circumstances required. He was a leader with strength and boldness and with the tenderness of love. His leadership is a perfect example of what leadership should be in every home. A husband leader imitates Christ and lead by example. Christ loved the father and also loved the church, yet the father was his first love. Until a husband takes the lead to seek first the kingdom none of his leadership skills would be effective in marriage. As a husband, your heart should anchor on God's word and not to emotions.

A husband leader puts God first in his marriage and does not forget God's word in every circumstance. A husband leader strives to be just in all his decisions by respecting God's word. A husband leader does not throw away his wife's opinions or suggestions because he is the head; but weighs every advice and counsel, because some circumstances require just moral principle or technical approach and not spiritual approach. There is no doubt about it that God can use a wife to inform her husband but, the husband is the responsible one that will first give account to God.

When God came to the garden, Adam was the one He called not Eve. Genesis 3:9 says, the Lord God called unto Adam, and said unto him, where art thou? He did not call the woman because Adam was the responsible one not Eve.

A HUSBAND'S DUTY TO THE WIFE:

To love a wife without condition and reservation is a husband's duty. Many husbands especially in Africa take it upon themselves to enforce their wives submission, forsaking their own duties, but husbands were not told to bend their wives.

The scripture says husband love your wife as Christ loved the church. Christ's love is sacrificial and without reservation but not without the interest of the father. True love depicts the fear of God and compassion. Genuine love produces good understanding and the fear of the Lord.

The love of Christ took him to the cross and that was the will of the father. The love of a husband for his wife will also involve a similar submission to Christ in the same manner Christ submitted to the father, a husband must submit to God. Christ love for the church did not take him away from the will of the father. Therefore, a husband's love for his wife should not take him away from the will of God. Husbands are to love their wives with Christ kind of love. Husbands are expected to love their wives as themselves, by caring for their wives as they care for themselves. Christ's kind of love is not worldly but love which produces holiness. Agape is the work of the Holy Spirit from within. Husband leaders love their wives and also fear God alongside with their love.

WIVES ROLE IN MARRIAGE

A wife is a married woman in relation to her husband. A wife is a female spouse with precious responsibilities. She is a woman with the role of being a mother, a wife, a keeper of the home, discreet, sober and spiritually minded for her entire household.

A virtuous woman uses her inspiration from God's word to place the needs of her husband above her own needs. Submitting to her husband according to God's will as the church is to Christ.

A virtuous woman keeps the secret of her intimate family away from other people. She is open to her husband and does not gossip to others about him, but reverences her husband and encourages him to be more Christ like in his actions.

She is devoted to domestic duties such as cooking and managing every household affair. Though a husband can help where help is needed but, God has given this role to the woman.

GENESIS 18:6 And Abraham hastened into the tent unto Sarah, and said, make ready quickly three measures of fine meal, knead it, and make cake upon the hearth.

A virtuous woman understands that her body belongs to her husband and wouldn't withhold herself from him sexually. She is motivated by the love of Christ and strives to model Christ through compassion, faithfulness, meekness, sobriety and holy discretion. She is faithful to God and to man and wouldn't make any attempt to topple her own husband in any aspect of their marriage.

She understands the word submission and wouldn't take the lead, thereby encouraging her husband not to neglect his leadership responsibility, but take it up and be more Christ like in his leadership.

Chapter 17
PROBLEMS AFFECTING MARRIAGES

There are problems facing many marriages everywhere, and most of these problems are human faults, while others are basically spiritual problems. Negative ethnic cultural influences are capable of turning a good marriage into a bad one. The system influences the lives of many married converts negatively and these bad influences can lead to lack of fulfillment in marriage. The marital lives of many converts are not influenced by God's word but by their own ethnic cultures and traditions.

Many Christian spouses strive to keep God's word yet encounter serious marital problems, while others do not have much time to obey God's command yet, they experience little problem though, many still have serious marital problems.

Problems facing many Christian marriages everywhere are mostly attacks of the devil. This is more reason Christian spouses should be spiritually sensitive everyday because the enemy hates holy matrimony. Problems that lead to dissolution of many marriages are mostly satanic attacks. Frankly speaking, every marriage experience attacks of the devil, but all don't suffer same weight of tribulations.

Temptations of this life are weapons Satan uses to persecute marriages, though temptation differs. Sarah suggested Haggai to Abraham, and also requested he should eject her and child out of home, was an annoying experience in their marriage. Isaac loved Esau and Rebecca preferred Jacob was also a serious temptation, and a difficult experience in their marriage.

Satan has many weapons that he uses to fight marriage, and flesh happens to be the vessel that carries these weapons of the devil. The flesh hates holiness and desire worldliness and corruption, but the Christian does not yield to desires of the flesh. Weapons Satan uses to attack marriages includes: Lack of self-control, lack of respect, materialism, negative media influences, Negative ethnic influences, financial issues, and lack of good marital intimacy.

1. **Lack of self-control:**

Marriage where there is no self control, flesh may rule in that marriage. Christian Spouses who know how to subdue flesh and bring it under control at all time do not struggle to fulfill purpose in marriage. Lack of self control is work of the flesh and sin against God. A situation where flesh rules in marriage, the ultimate purpose of matrimony may not be realized.

Self control involves holy conduct, forbearance, and good understanding. Self-control is fruit of the Spirit and it takes help of the Holy Spirit to have it on daily basis. The Christian yields daily to yearnings of the Spirit, and this submission to God produces self-control. The Holy Spirit helps the Christian to have self-control from the inward, as long the Christian submits daily to the Spirit.

2. **Lack of respect:**

If spouses lack respect for each other, their marriage may suffer many problems. The atmosphere of openness and closeness wouldn't be there in the marriage. If husband and wife lack respect for each other, they create loopholes for the devil to launch attacks into their marriage.

Lack of respect in marriage is capable of inviting sorrowful feelings, and series of problems that may lead to marital failure. Though respect is reciprocal however, God still expect the man and woman to understand very well their God given roles in marriage for better reciprocation of respect. Respect that involves the fear of God and obedience to Christ' commandments, can make a God fearing home. The Bible says, husband love your wife; wife submit to your own husband. Love produces respect and submission depicts respect. Respect that is accompanied by obedience to God's command and fear of the Lord is better than worldly kind of respect.

3. **Materialism:**

Materialism is excessive regard for worldly concerns. Materialism is a spirit. This evil spirit has caused many modern converts to believe salvation of the Christian revolves round earthly achievements and values of this life.

Materialism opposes holiness of Christ and keeps people in bondage of their own flesh. If a husband or wife suddenly becomes a material person; this may invite serious problem in the marriage. If a spouse is a material person it can result to serious issue with his or her spouse in relation. Materialism leads to wasteful extravagant lifestyle and is capable of breaking home if a spouse or both spouses are materialistic.

Genuine Christians are heaven conscious and spiritually minded even in marriage. They seek God's kingdom on daily basis; resisting lust, greed, and pride of this life. Excessive regard for earthly values can lead to a wasteful extravagant lifestyle and marital failure.

4. **Negative media influences:**

Many modern spouses live their lives as influenced by movies, magazines, and books. They read, listen, and view things that are capable of influencing their lives either positively or negatively. If Christian couples welcome every idea and lifestyles they see on movies, magazines, and books, forsaking God's word; their union may lack virtue and thereby lead to lack of fulfillment in Christ.

God established matrimony and called it holy, yet many marriages are not holy due to negative media influences everywhere. Many Christian spouses practice very well what they learn from media daily, and these ideas could be good or rather bad behaviors. Ideas from media are not sufficient to make a good home. Matured converts gets married to God's word alongside with their spouses.

5. **Negative Ethnic Influences:**

Ethnic cultures and traditions influence the lives of over 90% of married people in this world. In this modern world, many Christian spouses choose to ignore sound Biblical doctrine about marriage and follow ethnic cultures and traditions. Though ethnic cultures and traditions could make some positive impacts in marriage, but also make much negative impacts at same time.

Negative ethnic cultural influences invite serious problems in marriages. Apart from ethnic cultural influences; friends and family members also influences marriage either positively or negatively. If the Christian spouse place ethnic culture or tradition above biblical standard and discipline, God is not honored.

6. **Financial issues:**

If husband and wife conform properly to their God given roles in marriage, problem such as financial issues may not arise. Some financial issues in many marriages require technical approach as solution. If husband care for his own wife in same manner he cares for himself, and learn to sacrifice for her as scripture says; problem such financial issues may not arise in the marriage. And if wife through knowledge from God's word learn to place her husband's needs above her own needs; submitting unto her own husband as scripture says financial issues may not arise in her marriage.

If a husband takes the lead in his marital home, by loving his wife as the scripture requires of him, and wife through the fear of the Lord reverences her own husband as scripture commands; financial issues may not rise in their marriage.

7. Lack of good intimacy:

Lack of marital intimacy is a serious problem facing many marriages everywhere in the world. Though, intimacy means different things to different people in this world. However, intimacy that is in accord with God's will is the best among intimacies.

Good marital intimacy begins with the fear of the Lord and obedience to God's word. God ordained marriage in Eden and initiated the first marital intimacy between the first man and woman. This is more reason couples should fear God and submit to His will.

GENESIS 2:18 And the LORD God said, It is not good that the man should be alone; I will make him an help meet for him.

Many Christian marriages lack good marital intimacy because they first lack agape as foundational love. Holy matrimony is not worldly it involves the love of God, the fear of the Lord, and obedience to God's word.

Most marriages everywhere suffer unhealthy intimacies. The root of these problems must first be addressed before relationships can move forward to a healthier level. Factors that may lead to these unhealthy intimacies include: early sexual abuse, early exposure to sex, sexual addiction; regular loss of appetite for sex, constant misunderstanding, and above all, lack of agape as foundational love in marriage.

Agape is the work of the Holy Spirit and it begins with new heart from God. The Holy Spirit can heal every emotional wounds and psychological injuries in people's lives. The Holy Spirit helps Christian spouses to overcome every traumata of this life. There are no emotional wounds the Holy Spirit cannot heal. Agape helps Christian spouses move forward to that joyous level in marriage. Through help of the Holy Spirit, many Christian spouses still experience good marital intimacies.

The Strait Gate

Peter Mathias

www.ingramcontent.com/pod-product-compliance
Lightning Source LLC
Chambersburg PA
CBHW052059110526
44591CB00013B/2274